SENTENCE STRUCTURE

Second Edition

'This new edition retains the cardinal virtue of clarity: in its style, its progression, its terminology and its theoretical origins and loyalty. Further, it makes connections with dialect and discourse which set grammar in a broader context. And through its extended incremental guide to drawing syntactic trees, it is even better adapted to independent study.'

Tim Parke, University of Hertfordshire, UK

Routledge Language Workbooks provide absolute beginners with practical introductions to core areas of language study. Books in the series provide comprehensive coverage of the area as well as a basis for further investigation. Each Language Workbook guides the reader through the subject using 'hands-on' language analysis, equipping them with the basic analytical skills needed to handle a wide range of data. Written in a clear and simple style, with all technical concepts fully explained, Language Workbooks can be used for independent study or as part of a taught class.

Sentence Structure

- introduces the evidence for sentence structure and reveals its purpose
- is based on a problem-solving approach to language
- teaches the reader how to identify word classes, such as nouns, prepositions and demonstratives
- uses simple tree structures to analyse sentences
- contains numerous exercises to encourage practical skills of sentence analysis
- includes a database and exercises that compare the structure of English with other languages

This second edition of *Sentence Structure* has been fully revised and updated throughout and includes new material on tense, aspect, modality and the verb phrase, whilst the order of topics has been rearranged to improve clarity.

Nigel Fabb is Professor of Literary Linguistics at the University of Strathclyde in Glasgow. His publications include *A Grammar of Ma'di* (with Mairi Blackings, 2003) and *Language and Literary Structure* (2002).

LANGUAGE WORKBOOKS

Series editor: Richard Hudson

Books in the series:

SENTENCE STRUCTURE

Second Edition

NIGEL FABB

Routledge
Taylor & Francis Group

LONDON AND NEW YORK

First published 1994
by Routledge

Reprinted 1995, 1997, 2000, 2001, 2002

Second edition first published 2005
by Routledge
2 Park Square, Milton Park, Abingdon, Oxon OX14 4RN

Simultaneously published in the USA and Canada
by Routledge
270 Madison Ave, New York, NY 10016

Reprinted 2006, 2008

Routledge is an imprint of the Taylor & Francis Group, an informa business

© 1994, 2005 Nigel Fabb

Typeset in Galliard and Futura by
Florence Production Limited, Stoodleigh, Devon
Printed and bound in Great Britain by
TJ International Ltd, Padstow, Cornwall

British Library Cataloguing in Publication Data
A catalogue record for this book is available from the British
Library

Library of Congress Cataloging in Publication Data
A catalog record for this book has been requested

ISBN10: 0–415–34181–7 (hbk)
ISBN10: 0–415–34182–5 (pbk)

ISBN13: 978–0–415–34181–3 (hbk)
ISBN13: 978–0–415–34182–0 (pbk)

CONTENTS

ACKNOWLEDGEMENTS

The contributions by others to the first edition of this book remain relevant, and I thank again Woohak Lee, Toh Guat Choon, Kon Yoon How, Mairi John Blackings, Wan Faiezah bt. Megat Noordin, Yasmin bt. Osman, Rajathilagam a/l Krishnan, Deborah Cameron, Helen Reid-Thomas, Barbara MacMahon, Janet Fabb, Andrew Ing, Edward Waldron, Nurul Basher, Jillbob Newton, and the series editor, Dick Hudson. In preparing the second edition, I have benefited from some anonymous reviews, specific suggestions by Melissa Axelrod, Bob Morris-Jones and Jonathan Hope, and helpful editing by Kate Parker and Christabel Kirkpatrick at Routledge. I thank the students at Strathclyde University (Department of English Studies) who have used this book for the past ten years. This book is a summary of other people's discoveries, unacknowledged by name, and I thank them now.

USING THIS BOOK

This book teaches you how to identify classes of word such as noun, adverb and demonstrative, and it shows you how to work out the structure of a sentence by drawing a tree structure. The book assumes that you start out with no knowledge of grammar or linguistics.

Because the book teaches you practical skills, you should try to do the exercises. Some exercises get you to practise the structures learned in the chapters. Many exercises introduce concepts and structures which are not mentioned in the chapter text. You should write down the answers and draw tree structures where possible. An exercise with ☞ has answers or suggestions at the end of the book.

In this second edition I make explicit use of the verb phrase. Hence tree structures differ from those in the first edition.

ABBREVIATIONS

*	ungrammatical sentence
A	adjective
Adv	adverb
AdvP	adverb phrase
AP	adjective phrase
art	article
cc	coordinating conjunction
deg	degree modifier
dem	demonstrative
inf	infinitive marker
N	noun (including pronoun)
neg	negation
NP	noun phrase
num	numeral
P	preposition
PP	preposition phrase
Q	quantifier
S	sentence (both root sentence and subordinate clause)
sc	subordinating conjunction
V	verb
V_{aux}	auxiliary verb
V_{mod}	modal verb
VP	verb phrase

PHRASES

1

> A single written sentence may stand for two different sentence structures, each having a different meaning. The structures differ because the words are grouped into different phrases. Phrases can be discovered by replacement and movement of sequences of words.

What you already know about a sentence is that it is a sequence of words, starting with a capital letter, and ending with a full stop. When you have come to the end of this book, you will have a very different understanding of what a sentence is, and what it is made of. This understanding was traditionally called an understanding of grammar. In linguistic theory it is the understanding of SYNTAX, which is the structure of the sentence. **Syntax** It will require some work to achieve this understanding; here are the reasons which I think make it worth the trouble.

- The ability to speak or write by constructing the complex objects which are sentences is something that only humans can do. Other animals can communicate, but sentence structure is beyond them. By studying sentences we study ourselves. Whereas grammar was once a matter of learning by rote, now – and in this book – it is a science, based on experiment and exploration.
- All humans have language, but we are divided by our languages and our dialects. One of the goals of this book is to understand how languages and dialects differ, with the broader goal of understanding how, fundamentally, they are the same. The knowledge of language which linguists have tends to make them more tolerant of linguistic diversity; this can only be a good thing.
- Linguistics – the study of language – is applied in many domains, including medical, social, legal, literary, anthropological, and historical studies. The understanding of how sentences work is the first step towards being able to participate in these applications of language.

MEANING AND PHRASE STRUCTURE

The sentence in (1) has two different meanings: it is ambiguous.

    (1)   I was reading the letter to John.

►   **Before you read any further, decide what the two alternative meanings of this sentence are.**

This sentence might mean:

    (2)   There was a letter addressed to John which I was reading (perhaps to myself).

Or it might mean:

    (3)   There was a letter (to me, perhaps) which I was reading aloud to John.

How does one sequence of words produce two different and alternative meanings? The answer is that the sequencing of words does not by itself produce a meaning; instead there is a hidden organization of the words which gives them their meaning. For the sequence of words in (1) there are two alternative organizations of the words, each of which delivers a different meaning: because the ambiguity is based on two different **Structural** structures for the same sequence of words this is called a STRUCTURAL **ambiguity** AMBIGUITY. As people who understand English, we know the two alternative organizations implicitly because we are able to understand the two meanings, and this means that we are unconsciously organizing the words either one way or another. The organization of a sentence is its **Syntactic** SYNTACTIC STRUCTURE, and in this book you will learn how to draw a **structure** diagram of the syntactic structure of a sentence which you unconsciously already know – as a central part of your ability to speak and write.

The words in (1) are visibly laid out on the page like beads on a string. To understand how this string of words can produce two different meanings we must say that they are invisibly organized into groups. We might think of the words as put into boxes, all contained within the sentence which is the biggest box of all.

    (4)   I was reading the | letter to John. |

    (5)   I was reading the | letter to | | John. |

Phrase   A 'box' of words is called a PHRASE. In (4) the sequence of words *the letter to John* forms a single phrase, while in (5) the sequence is broken up into two phrases: *the letter* forms one phrase and *to John* forms another separate one. This explains why a sentence can have two different meanings, because the same string of words can be grouped in two different ways, and each grouping relates to a meaning.

It is often useful to think about the relation between a phrase and something in the world which it represents. In the case of (4) the grouping *the letter to John* names a specific object, a letter whose characteristic is that it is (addressed) to John. In the case of (5) the object represented is just *the letter* and the words *to John* do not help to identify that object.

REPLACEMENT AND PHRASE STRUCTURE

A sentence has a syntactic structure which is hidden from view but which can be revealed by various tests. In this section you will learn a simple test (6) which will reveal some of the phrases in the sentence.

> (6)   TEST: REPLACEMENT BY *IT*
> If a sequence of words can be replaced by the word *it* without significantly changing the meaning, then that sequence of words is a phrase.

If the test is applied to the sentence in (1), we see that there are two alternatives – either the sequence *the letter to John* is replaced by *it* and hence is a phrase, or the sequence *the letter* is replaced by *it* and hence is a phrase. The two alternative possibilities of replacement give two sentences with different groupings into phrases (7) and (8), and which each have a single clear meaning.

> (7)   I was reading   it.

Phrase (7) means (2) (the letter is addressed to John)

> (8)   I was reading   it   to John.

Phrase (8) means (3) (implying that John hears it being read)

The relation between these and the boxed versions of the sentences is clear. In (7), *it* replaces the boxed sequence in (4), and this organization of the sentence corresponds to the meaning whereby *the letter to John* describes an object, a letter addressed to John. And in (8), *it* replaces the boxed sequence *the letter* in (5), with the other meaning.

Replacement is possible because the word *it* is the same kind of thing as the sequence of words [*the letter to John*] or the sequence of words [*the letter*]. All three are a specific kind of phrase called a noun phrase.

In box terms, there is a box labelled 'noun phrase' which can contain *it* or *the letter to John* or *the letter*. So we are replacing like for like, with the word *it* being a minimal or stripped-down noun phrase standing for **Pronoun** a more filled-out noun phrase. *It* is called a PRONOUN, though it should more properly be called a pro-noun-phrase because it substitutes for a noun phrase. Other pronouns can also substitute for noun phrases – some of the pronouns of English are listed below.

> Some pronouns:
> *it, she, her, hers, he, him, his, they, them, their, theirs, I, my, mine, you, your, yours, we, our, ours.*

▶ **The pronoun *him* can also substitute for part of the sentence in (1). Which part can it substitute for, and what does that tell us about that part of the sentence?**

MOVEMENT AND PHRASE STRUCTURE

Words stick together when they are in the same phrase – they can be picked up and moved together. Again, a phrase is like a box of words within the sentence, which can be picked up and carried somewhere else. We can formulate another test (9) for constituency.

> (9) THE MOVEMENT TEST
> If a sequence of words can be moved together, then that sequence of words is a phrase.

We know that the sentence in (1) contains either the phrase *the letter* or the phrase *the letter to John*, and we can move either of these to the beginning of the sentence, at the same time, rewriting the sentence to remove *I*, the reader.

> (10) The letter to John was being read.

> (11) The letter was being read to John.

Like replacement, movement forces a choice on us – we have to decide which of the two possible phrase structures (4) or (5) is the right one, and move a phrase/box accordingly. Once have moved the phrase we have removed the source of the ambiguity, which was the fact that a string of words *the letter to John* could be put into phrases in two different ways.

APPLYING THE TESTS

We have seen two loose tests or rules of thumb for the discovery of syntactic structure. The replacement test (6) discovers a phrase of a particular kind by replacing it with a stripped-down phrase of the same kind. It was formulated specifically using a pronoun, which is a ready-made minimal noun phrase. We can generalize to get another test (12).

> (12) THE REPLACEMENT TEST
> A phrase containing several words can sometimes be substituted by a phrase of the same kind containing a single word, while maintaining a related meaning.

Consider for example (13) which can be rewritten as (14), with a clearly related, though less specific meaning.

> (13) John seems to be very happy with his new bathroom.

> (14) John seems to be happy.

The possibility of substituting *very happy with his new bathroom* with the single word *happy* arises because both are the same kind of phrase – both are adjective phrases. Thus the replacement test as formulated in (12) shows that *very happy with his new bathroom* is a phrase.

▶   **Use the movement test (9) to double-check that *very happy with his new bathroom* is a phrase.**

A PHRASE CAN CONTAIN ANOTHER PHRASE

A sentence is a sequence of words which are organized into phrases; we visualized this by saying that words were in boxes inside the big box of the sentence. But phrases can also be inside phrases – that is, the sentence can contain boxes which contain boxes which contain words. We know that *very happy with his new bathroom* is a phrase. But the movement test tells us that *with his new bathroom* is also a phrase inside the larger one.

> (15) With his new bathroom, John seems to be very happy.

And the replacement test tells us that *his new bathroom* is also a phrase:

> (16) John seems to be very happy with it.

These tests suggest that the box structure of the sentence, showing its phrases inside phrases, is partially something like this:

(17)

John seems to be (very happy (with (his new bathroom.)))

▶ There are three noun phrases in (13). Identify them.

Working out the phrase structure of a sentence consists largely of working out how words group into phrases, and working out how phrases fit into other phrases, as in the example above.

UNGRAMMATICALITY

When a sentence fails a test, we learn something from it. For example, we might move *very happy with* to the beginning of the sentence to see if the words stick together as a phrase.

(18) * Very happy with John seems to be his new bathroom.

Ungrammatical

The rules of the language do not permit this sentence to exist, and so we call it UNGRAMMATICAL and we symbolize this by putting an asterisk in front of it. Linguists who want to test the limits of a language do so by finding out which sentences are ungrammatical, and try to explain why.

The notion of 'ungrammatical' should be distinguished from some more general notion of 'unacceptable'. Sentences might be grammatical by the rules of the language or dialect; but grammatical sentences might nevertheless be considered unacceptable for various reasons. One reason for deciding that a sentence is unacceptable is because it breaks some invented rule of 'proper language', such as the rule invented for English that a sentence should not end on a preposition. These invented rules

Prescriptive rules

are called PRESCRIPTIVE RULES. Prescriptive rules are not descriptions of what is or is not possible structurally in the language; instead they are attempts to control a speaker's or writer's behaviour.

EXERCISES

1.1 ☞ Structural ambiguities

Each sentence below has two possible meanings because each sentence is structurally ambiguous.

(19) Peter untied the parcel for Toby.

(20) Kes pushed the ping-pong ball under the sofa.

(21) I drove the visitor from Glasgow.

(a) Use the test of replacement by *it* or some other pronoun to discover where the noun phrases are. Different versions of each sentence should give you different results.

(b) Use the movement test to do the same thing. For each sentence you should find that there are two possible ways of using movement to disambiguate (= remove the ambiguity).

1.2 ☞ The replacement and movement tests

(a) Use the replacement test to find out whether *the book tomorrow* is one phrase or two separate phrases in the following sentence.

(22) I will read the book tomorrow.

(b) Does the movement test give you the same result? Bear in mind that you can do several different movements within this same sentence.

1.3 Knowledge of phrases

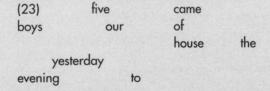

(23)   five   came
boys   our   of
                  house   the
     yesterday
evening   to

Make a grammatical English sentence from this jumble of words. As you do so, write down a description of:

(a) how you know how to group the words together into phrases; try to do this without mentioning word classes ('verb' etc.), even if you know them;

(b) how you decide how the phrases are ordered to make a sentence; try to do this without mentioning phrase classes (such as 'noun phrase'), even if you know them.

1.4 ☞ Identifying phrases in Korean

The acceptable Korean sentences (24)–(28) below all mean roughly the same thing: 'Yesterday the old man gave Peter's green ball to the children.'

(a) Circle what you think the phrases are in the first of these sentences (24), on the basis of the evidence provided by the reordered other sentences.

> (24) Eaje ke noin-i chorok saek kong-el peter-ei aidel-ege ju-eatsepnida.

> (25) Ke noin-i eaje chorok saek kong-el peter-ei aidel-ege ju-eatsepnida.

> (26) Eaje ke noin-i peter-ei aidel-ege chorok saek kong-el ju-eatsepnida.

> (27) Chorok saek kong-el ke noin-i peter-ei aidel-ege eaje ju-eatsepnida.

> (28) Peter-ei aidel-ege ke noin-i eaje chorok saek kong-el ju-eatsepnida.

(b) Is it better to say that Korean has 'free word order' or that it has 'free phrase order'?

This activity demonstrates that it is possible to find the phrase structure of a sentence without knowing much about the meaning of the individual phrases. Korean is a language which allows fairly free order, but you will have noticed that one part is always final – this is the verb: here, *ju-eatsepnida*, meaning 'gave'.

1.5 ☞ Unacceptable or ungrammatical?

Here are some sentences. They fall into three classes:

(a) grammatical in all dialects of English;

(b) grammatical in some dialects of English but not others;

(c) ungrammatical in all dialects of English.

For each sentence, try to decide which class it falls into. This will probably involve some guessing, since you will not be familiar with all dialects of English.

> (29) And think of the music of his pipe.

> (30) The moon is made of green cheese.

> (31) We canny be sure o' that.

(32) He's the one that I wanted to read the book to.

(33) I done it yesterday.

(34) Peter asked Mary to show himself the picture.

(35) Who did you see Peter and?

(36) I am seeing the sky from here.

(37) It was useless, totally fucking useless.

(38) He is might going.

1.6 Working with other languages

The following longer exercise requires you to work with the four corpora at the end of the book. As you work, you will find it useful to put word-for-word translations under the sentences (this slows you down, but it will be increasingly useful as you go through the book). You may find that you can't translate all the words to start with (for example the Malay word *telah* may prove difficult); leave these problems – you will get a chance to focus on them in later chapters. Read 'How to use the four corpora which follow' (pp. 93–4) before doing this exercise.

The purpose of this exercise is to give you further practice at using the tests for phrases, and to demonstrate some of the differences in phrase structure between different languages. By comparing sentences which mean similar things in a language it is possible to detect the presence of phrases, because phrases can be moved or replaced. The following sets of sentences demonstrate the presence of phrases. For each language's set, say what evidence there is for the presence of phrases in the sentence. We have given a sample answer to (a):

(a)   Chinese: compare B1, 2, 3

Sample answer: *sai louchai* can be replaced by *pinko*, suggesting that it is a phrase. *kó teeu tai yu* can be replaced by *matye*, suggesting that it is a phrase.

(b)   Chinese: compare C1, C2

(c)   Madi: compare B1, B2, B4–6

(d)   Madi: compare C3 with C4 and C1 with C2 (make sure you read the notes at the beginning of the Madi section)

(e)   Madi: compare A2, L1 and L2; compare A3, L3 and L4

(f)   Malay: compare C1, C2

(g)   Malay: compare B1–5

(h) Malay: compare A1–3 with L1–3

(i) Tamil: compare A1, A2

(j) Tamil: compare B1, B3 (replacement)

(k) Tamil: compare B1–10 (movement)

WORD CLASS AND PHRASE CLASS

2

The noun phrase

Each word belongs to a word class, which determines its position. The position of a word in the sentence depends not on its linear position but instead on its place within a phrase.

WORD CLASS

Every word belongs to a WORD CLASS, such as noun, verb, adjective, article, conjunction, etc. Other names for word class are 'category' or 'part of speech'. Here is a list of the word classes we discuss in this book.

Word class

Symbol	Class name	Examples
A	adjective	*rapid, blue, impossible, ultraviolet, frozen, edible, African, tiny, lovely, comical, unbelievable, snowy, former*
Adv	adverb	*well, fortunately, possibly, quickly, fast, sadly, soon, improbably, standardly, pompously, hopelessly*
art	article	*the, a, an*
cc	coordinating conjunction	*and, or*
deg	degree modifier	*very, quite, rather, somewhat, more, most, much*
dem	demonstrative	*this, that, these, those*
inf	infinitive marker	*to*
N	noun	*table, action, box, unicorn, emptiness, Napoleon, postman, love, door, law, Scotland, Renaissance, cuckoo-clock*
N	a subclass of nouns – the pronouns	*I, me, my, you, your, he, him, his, she, her, hers, we, us, our, they, them, their, it, its, himself*

neg	negation	*not*
num	numeral	*one, two, fifteen, a million and two*
P	preposition	*in, on, under, over, before, into, between, to, at, beneath, for, of*
Q	quantifier	*every, some, all, few, most, much, no, many*
sc	subordinating conjunction	*that, because, whether, if*
V	verb	*kiss, collapse, emphasize, vanish, be, deodorize, die, sit, exist, melt, build, table, vacuum-clean, window-shop*
V_{aux}	auxiliary verb	*have, be, do*
V_{mod}	modal verb	*might, could, must, should, will, shall*

In this chapter we will see why putting words into word classes helps us understand their behaviour.

THE ORDER OF WORDS IS DEPENDENT ON PHRASE STRUCTURE

Linguists investigate sentence structure by inventing sentences, making small changes to them, and watching what happens. This means that the study of language belongs to the scientific tradition of using experiments to understand some part of our world. For example, if we make up a sentence (1) and then make a small change to it to get (2), we find that the second sentence is ungrammatical, as indicated by the asterisk.

(1)　I saw the white house.

(2)　* I saw the house white.

Why? One possibility is that it relates to the words themselves; perhaps the word *white* and the word *house* must always come in this order. But if we were to explain in this way we would need separate explanations for a very large number of words, including the words in the sentences in (3)–(6), which show the same pattern.

(3)　He read the new book.

(4)　* He read the book new.

(5)　We fed some hungry dogs.

(6)　* We fed some dogs hungry.

These sentences show us that whatever principle gives us the order of words, it must be based on the class of word, not on a specific word. The words *white, new* and *hungry* are all a class of word called an adjective; the words *house, book* and *dogs* are all a class of word called a noun. We could formulate a generalization, which holds true for the sentences in (1)–(6).

(7)   An adjective cannot immediately follow a noun.

A GENERALIZATION is a statement which remains true for lots of examples, and a generalization such as (7) is an attempt to explain the principles by which a sentence is put together. One of the useful consequences of a generalization is to make a prediction which can then be tested, and if the prediction turns out to be wrong, then the generalization can be improved. Our generalizations summarize our understanding of language, and by improving our generalizations we increase our understanding of how sentences work. The generalization in (7) makes a prediction which turns out to be wrong, when we look at sentence (8).

Generalization

(8)   I painted the house white.

Why is (8) grammatical when (2) is not, given that both end on the same sequence of *house white*? The answer is the most important thing to know about sentence structure, so important that we give it its own paragraph:

> The grammaticality of a sentence depends not on the sequence of words but how the words are combined into phrases.

▶   **Use the replacement test to find where the noun phrases are in (1) and (2) and (8).**

What you will find is that in (1) the adjective and the noun are in the same phrase, a noun phrase as demonstrated by the fact that *the white house* can be replaced by *it*.

(1)   I saw the white house.

(9)   I saw it.

In contrast, in (8) the noun and the adjective are in different phrases. The noun phrase is just *the house* and the adjective *white* follows the noun phrase and is not inside the noun phrase.

(8)   I painted the house white.

(10) I painted it   white.

This suggests that we take our incorrect generalization (7) and rewrite it as an improved generalization (11).

(11) An adjective cannot immediately follow a noun when they are both in the same noun phrase.

One of the useful things about our generalizations is that they allow us to make a very specific comparison between English and another language. For example, while in English the adjective comes before the noun within the noun phrase, this is not true in Welsh, as the following examples show:

(12)   *y   gwyn   tŷ
        the   white   house
        the white house

(13)   y   tŷ   gwyn
        the   house   white
        the white house

(14)   *newydd llyfr   Mary
        new   book   Mary
        Mary's new book

(15)   llyfr   newydd Mary
        book   new   Mary
        Mary's new book

These sentences suggest that while generalization (11) is true for English, for Welsh we should formulate generalization (16).

(16) (Welsh:) An adjective cannot immediately precede a noun when they are both in the same noun phrase.

Returning to English, we know that the three words [*the white house*] together constitute a noun phrase, because they can be substituted by *it*. We have seen that *white* precedes *house* because an adjective precedes a noun. What about the word *the*? This word is a member of a very small **Article** word class, the class ARTICLE (the other member is the word *a* which has an alternative form *an*). In English, an article must come at the beginning of a noun phrase, as the following alternatives show.

(17) I saw the white house.

(18) * I saw white the house.

(19) * I saw white house the.

We could formulate a generalization (20).

(20) An article must come at the beginning of a noun phrase.

What is important here is that there is no possibility of explaining the position of the article without making it relative to the noun phrase. We cannot for example say that an article cannot follow an adjective, because sentences such as (21) are grammatical.

(21) I painted white the ceiling and red the walls.

▶ **Why can the article *the* follow the adjective in (21) but not in (18)?**

Our generalization in (20) is true for English, and for Welsh. But it is not true for the West African language Fon, spoken in Benin and neighbouring countries, and also called Fongbe. As (22) shows, in Fon the article must come at the end of the noun phrase, a generalization stated in (23).

(22) vi   o
      child   the
      the child

(23) (Fon:) An article must come at the end of a noun phrase.

HOW TO IDENTIFY A NOUN, ARTICLE AND ADJECTIVE

In the previous section I assumed perhaps incorrectly that you knew what a noun, adjective and article were. Since the purpose of this book is to give you ways of finding things out about sentence structure, now we look at some ways of discovering whether something is a noun, article or adjective. We start with articles: these are easy to identify because there are just two of them, *the* and *a* (with its alternative form *an*). Whenever you see one of these words you know both that it is an article and that it is at the beginning of a noun phrase.

It is not easy to invent a new article, so we say that it belongs to a CLOSED CLASS of words. In contrast, it is easy to invent a new noun, **Closed class**

Open class

so we say that it belongs to an OPEN CLASS of words. This means that you can't just learn all the nouns. Instead we need a way of testing whether a word is a noun or not, and we will use a test which looks at the shape of the word. The shape of a word, particularly the prefix or suffix it takes, is its MORPHOLOGY, and (24) is a morphological test.

Morphology

> (24) If a word can be made plural it is a noun. ('Making plural' usually involves adding the suffix -s but can also involve a change of shape, such as *man* > *men*.)

▶ **Try this test on the nouns listed at the beginning of this chapter. Does it work for all of them?**

What about adjectives? Adjectives are not quite as easy to test morphologically, but one test which often works for short adjectives is this.

> (25) An adjective can be made comparative by adding the suffix -er.

Another characteristic of many adjectives is that it is possible to put the word *very* in front of them. So for example the word *happy* can be made into *happier* and it is also possible to say *very happy*. The word passes both tests and is clearly an adjective. Neither test is fully reliable, however, and also while they help differentiate adjectives from nouns they do not differentiate adjectives from another word class – adverbs – because both tests also work for adverbs.

▶ **Try these tests on the adjectives listed at the beginning of this chapter. Do both tests work for all of them?**

TREE STRUCTURES

Constituent structure

In this chapter we have seen that the class of a word determines its position in a sentence and that this is relative to the sentence's CONSTITUENT STRUCTURE. The English noun phrases we have looked at are constituted of, or have as their constituents, an optional article followed by an optional adjective followed by a noun. The constituent structure of a phrase is conventionally represented in one of two ways – either as a tree structure as in (26) or a bracketed structure as in (27).

(26)

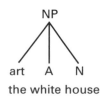

(27) [_{NP} [_{art} the] [_A white] [_N house]]

The tree structure takes up more space on the page but because it is so much easier to look at and immediately understand, I will generally use tree structures and suggest that you do so too. The relation between the tree structure and the bracketed structure should be clear: they are notational variants, which means that they vary only in how they are written out, not in any substantial way. Tree structures are usually written above the sentence, which means that the root of the tree is at the top and the 'leaves' (the words) are at the bottom.

EXERCISES

2.1 ☞ Adding new words

(a) Here is a list of word classes or subclasses. Fill in the empty columns if you can (you will not be able to in some cases).

(b) Which word classes are open and which are closed?

word class/ subclass	example word	word added in the past 10 years	plausible word which you invent
noun	*tractor*		
pronoun	*she*		
personal name	*Wendy*		
verb	*marmalize*		
adjective	*grubby*		
adverb	*flatteringly*		
preposition	*beyond*		
respect title	*Miss*		
article	*the*		
demonstrative	*these*		

2.2 Subclasses of noun

Here are two subclasses of words:

    (i)   time words: *today, tomorrow, yesterday*

    (ii) personal names: *Mary, Molly Brown*

For each subclass of words, show that the words in question are nouns. Do this by finding titles of books, films, television programmes, songs, etc. which incorporate these words and demonstrate that they are nouns. For example, the title of a television programme, *Tomorrow's World*, shows you that *tomorrow* is a noun, because it takes the possessive suffix *-s*.

2.3 Two adjectives in a noun phrase

The noun phrases we have looked at in this chapter all have at most one adjective before the noun. But it is possible to have two or more adjectives preceding the noun.

(a) Make up ten noun phrases which have two adjectives in them – such as [*the long hot summer*]. Try reversing the order of adjective phrases in each of these noun phrases to get for example [*the hot long summer*]. In reversed order does each of them sound just as good to you? For example, to me [*the hot long summer*] sounds odd.

(b) Try to find some generalizations: can you, for example, predict that a particular adjective will be first in a pair? Or that an adjective with one general kind of meaning (such as size) always precedes an adjective with another general kind of meaning?

2.4 ☞ Sound and word class

The sound of a word can systematically relate to its word class.

(a) The word *permit* can be a noun or a verb. They sound different; describe this difference. Find similar examples.

(b) Words beginning with the letters 'th' are pronounced with a voiced sound symbolized ð as in *the* or a voiceless sound symbolized θ as in *thin*. Try to find a generalization, relating to word class, which predicts how initial 'th' will be pronounced.

2.5 ☞ Numerals

What we are calling the 'word class' of numerals includes: *three*, *thirty*, *a thousand*, etc. This is not really a distinct word class; explain why.

WORD CLASS AND PHRASE CLASS **19**

2.6 Suffixes and word class

The following is a list of suffixed and prefixed words.

function-ary	*method-ist*
legend-ary	*profan-ity*
money-ed	*dead-ly*
reptil-ian	*ghost-ly*
librar-ian	*happi-ness*
peace-ful	*spac-ious*
nation-hood	*heart-y*
metall-ic	*robber-y*
boy-ish	*in-sane*
modern-ism	*un-sanitary*
despot-ism	*non-person*
formal-ist	

Show how the morphology of each word relates to its word class. Look at the class of the word to which the affix attaches and the class of the word which it creates; and ask whether there is a generalization, involving word class, for this affix.

3 MORE CLASSES OF PHRASE

Adjective phrase, adverb phrase and preposition phrase

> For some classes of word, there is an equivalent class of phrase. The word class heads the equivalent phrase class; for example, a noun is the head of a noun phrase.

THE PHRASE AND ITS HEAD

Why is a noun phrase called a 'noun' phrase, thereby associating the phrase as a whole with one of its constituents? There are various ways of answering this question, but they all circulate around the same basic idea – that the most important word in this phrase is the noun. The noun is the word which is least likely to be omitted. If we were to strip down a noun phrase to a single word, the word which would best capture its meaning would most likely be the noun. And the other constituents of the phrase can all be understood as serving the noun, in some sense. We **Head** say that the noun is the HEAD of the noun phrase. A phrase and its head share the same category: hence a noun is the head of a noun phrase. Except in unusual circumstances, whenever we find a noun we can always assume that it is the head of a noun phrase. The unusual circumstances are compounds, p. 50, and coordination, p. 49.

ADJECTIVE PHRASE

Other classes of words are also heads of phrases and are usually contained in their phrases. So for example an adjective is the head of an adjective phrase. This means that we need to rethink our tree structure for the noun phrase, so that if it contains an adjective then that adjective is in an adjective phrase rather than being just a bare adjective inside the noun phrase. We then restate the tree structure (26) from Chapter 2 as (1).

(1)

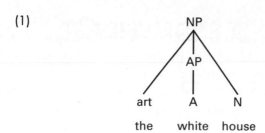

This is an improvement because it explains something about this phrase which otherwise cannot be explained. We can add the word *quite* to this phrase, but only if it is immediately followed by the word *white*:

(2)   The quite white house.

(3)   * The white quite house.

(4)   * The quite house.

The word *quite* belongs to the word class DEGREE MODIFIER. A degree modifier is positioned relative to an adjective, irrespective of the surrounding words, just as the article *the* is positioned relative to a noun, irrespective of the surrounding words. We can understand this by saying that *quite* and *white* are in the same adjective phrase, and that a degree modifier must come at the beginning of an adjective phrase.

Degree modifier

Chapter 2 began with a list of word classes. Does every class of word head its own phrase? This is a difficult question to answer and a matter of discussion in current linguistic theory, and impossible to answer in this short book. I will be making a simplifying assumption that only five classes of word head their own phrase: noun, adjective, adverb, preposition and verb. This means that the other classes of word are bare within a host phrase rather than heading a phrase of their own. The article appears only within a noun phrase, and the degree modifier mainly within an adjective phrase or adverb phrase. Thus one of the ways in which phrase classes are differentiated is that they contain different classes of bare word.

ADVERB PHRASE V. ADJECTIVE PHRASE

The degree modifier *quite* can appear inside an adjective phrase such as [*quite red*] and it can also appear inside an adverb phrase, such as [*quite quickly*], with the adverb *quickly*. In fact, the internal structure of adjective phrases is much like the internal structure of adverb phrases. Why then do we differentiate adjectives like *red* from adverbs like *quickly*?

One justification relates to word shape and structure: many adverbs end in -*ly* and relatively few adjectives do. But the crucial reason for differentiating them relates to the different positions in which we find adjective phrases in comparison with adverb phrases.

The phrase structure rule for a noun phrase says that an adjective phrase can be contained in a noun phrase. In contrast, an adverb phrase cannot, as is seen in (6).

(5)   The [AP quite quick] swimmer

(6)   *The [AdvP quite quickly] swimmer

Where, then, are adverb phrases found? A crude answer to this question is that adverb phrases most characteristically roam free in the sentence and without very major effects on the meaning of the sentence. As (10) shows, the adverb phrase cannot roam into the noun phrase.

(7)   Quite quickly I saw the swimmer.

(8)   I quite quickly saw the swimmer.

(9)   I saw quite quickly the swimmer.

(10)   *I saw the quite quickly swimmer.

(11)   I saw the swimmer quite quickly.

Here is a tree structure diagram for (8). I haven't yet explained about VP, the phrase which is headed by the verb; these are included in the diagrams and will be explained in Chapter 4.

(12)

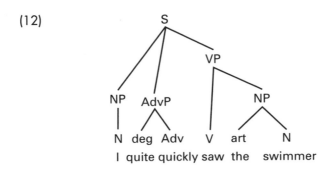

This distributive difference between adjective phrase and adverb phrase can be understood at least crudely by seeing the adjective phrase as telling us something about the noun or the noun phrase, and the adverb phrase as telling us something about the verb or about the event as a whole. *Quite quick* in (5) tells us about *the swimmer,* while *quite quickly* in the above sentence tells us about the event of seeing, as expressed by the verb *see.*

Adjective phrases are thus found inside noun phrases because they work with the noun phrase, while adverb phrases have no relation with the noun phrase as such and so are independent of it. Adjective phrases are also found outside noun phrases, in sentences like (13).

(13) The swimmer was quite quick.

(14)

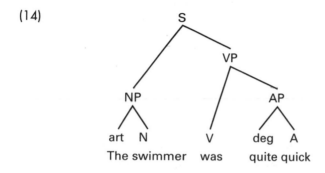

But even though it is outside the noun phrase, the adjective phrase here still tells us about the noun phrase and not about the verb or the event as a whole. When adjective phrases appear outside noun phrases they are not freely placed within the sentence; they do not roam free like adverb phrases, and this helps us differentiate them.

PREPOSITIONS AND PREPOSITION PHRASES

▶   There are three noun phrases in the following sentence. Use the test of replacement by a pronoun to determine which they are, and circle them.

(15) The woman gave the book to the man.

▶   But there is one other kind of phrase which we could also circle. Show, by reordering the sentence, that there is one more phrase so far uncircled and including several words.

It is possible to rewrite the sentence in a different order as (16) or (17):

(16) To the man the woman gave the book.

(17) The woman gave to the man the book.

So this movement test shows that [*to the man*] is a phrase, because the three words are moved around as a unit. What makes this phrase different from the other phrases we have looked at so far is that it contains **Preposition**   the word *to*, a word which belongs to the word class PREPOSITION.

The class of prepositions is closed. Some of the commonly found ones are: *in, on, to, of, by, about, under, over, between*. Most of them express location in space or time. A preposition is the head of a preposition phrase and usually comes before a noun phrase (hence pre-position).

In the sentences we have seen so far, preposition phrases are found outside the noun phrase and are independent of any particular noun phrase. However, a preposition phrase can also be inside the noun phrase and then tells us about the noun phrase. We saw this in Chapter 1, where our string of words [*I was reading the letter to John*] could be given two different phrasings. In one, the preposition phrase [*to John*] is inside the noun phrase headed by *letter* and it modifies *letter*; it is *the letter to John*. In the other, the preposition phrase [*to John*] is outside and so independent of the noun phrase [*the letter*].

(18)

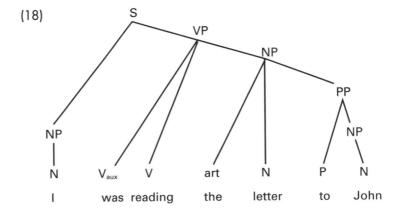

(19)

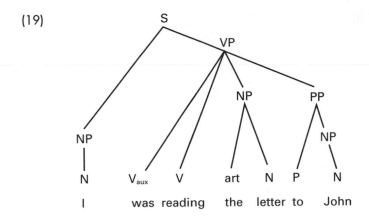

Preposition phrases are also found inside adjective phrases and adverb phrases. You can demonstrate this for yourself, using the following examples.

(20) I am proud of the painting.

(21) Unfortunately for him, the bill arrived.

▶ **Use tests of replacement and movement to discover and circle the adjective phrase in (20) and the adverb phrase in (21). Put boxes around the preposition phrases in each sentence; you should find that the preposition phrase is inside the adjective or adverb phrase.**

These are the tree structures.

(22)

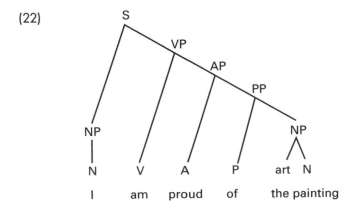

(23)

```
                              S
                          ╱  ╱│╲
                      AdvP ╱  │  ╲
                      ╱╲  ╱   │    ╲
                     ╱ PP    ╱     ╲
                    ╱  ╱╲   ╱       ╲
                   ╱  ╱  NP  NP      VP
                  ╱  ╱   │  ╱╲       │
                Adv  P   N art N      V
          Unfortunately for him,  the bill arrived
```

The most characteristic structure for a preposition phrase is to have a preposition as its head, followed by a noun phrase. In other kinds of phrase, it is usually possible to have just the head on its own and this is also possible in a preposition phrase.

(24) I put it down the drain.

(25) I put it down.

The sentence structure for (25) would be:

(26)

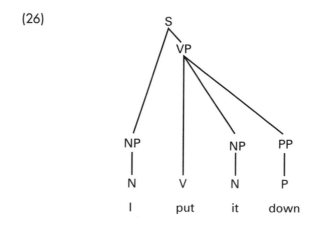

```
         S
        ╱╲
       ╱ VP
      ╱ ╱│╲╲
     ╱ ╱ │ ╲ ╲
    NP╱  │  NP PP
    │╱   │   │  │
    N    V   N  P
    I    put it down
```

Prepositions also have an unusual characteristic, which is that the preposition can be followed inside its phrase by another preposition phrase, as illustrated in (27) which has the tree structure in (28).

(27) I pulled the toys out of the box.

(28)

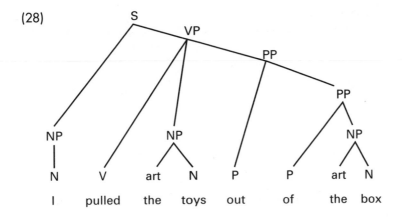

N I pulled the toys out of the box (tree diagram: S → NP[N: I], VP[V: pulled, NP[art: the, N: toys], PP[P: out, PP[P: of, NP[art: the, N: box]]]])

▶ Demonstrate by applying tests that [*out of the box*] is a single phrase.

EXERCISES

3.1 ☞ Practice: trees for AdvP

(29)–(33) are adverb phrases. Draw tree structures for them.
  (29) very quickly
  (30) somewhat reluctantly
  (31) willingly
  (32) happily for us
  (33) rather too speedily

3.2 ☞ Moving AdvP

Adverb phrases can appear in various different places in a sentence. Try putting the adverb phrase *violently* into the following sentence in every possible position. You should end up with nine variations. Which positions are unacceptable, and why?

  (34) The red car swerved out of the way.

3.3 ☞ Adjective or adverb?

(a) Is *fast* an adjective or an adverb?

(b) *quicker* is a comparative form, but is it a comparative form of the adjective *quick* or the adverb *quickly*?

(c) Some speakers of English would say *I quite quick saw the swimmer*. Which of the following would be correct as descriptions of what they are doing? Justify your answer.

(i) Speakers of this dialect are producing an ungrammatical sentence.

(ii) In this dialect, adjective phrases are permitted to modify verbs.

(iii) In this dialect, *quick* is an adverb.

3.4 ☞ Practice trees for PP

(35)–(40) are preposition phrases. Draw tree structures for them.

    (35) after the ball
    (36) down a nearby road
    (37) down
    (38) right down
    (39) out of the door
    (40) totally beside himself

3.5 ☞ The meaning of prepositions

Some prepositions can express location in time and location in space. For example *after* can do both: *after five o'clock* and *he ran after the bus*. Can all prepositions do this?

3.6 ☞ Preposition or particle?

In some grammars of English words such as *out*, *down* and *up* in sentences like (41)–(43) are called 'particles' (not prepositions). Why instead is it legitimate to classify these as prepositions, rather than invent a new word class?

    (41) The cat ran *out*.
    (42) She fell *down*.
    (43) They sent it *up*.

3.7 *Better than him*

Write a tree structure for the phrase '*better than him*'. You are likely to find this task difficult; I had phone calls from several readers of the first edition of this book asking me what the answer was. I suggest you follow these steps:

(a) Think up some sentences with the phrase *better than him* in them, and use this as a way – along with the various substitution and movement tests – of deciding what the phrase class is.

(b) Once you know the phrase class, decide which of these words is likely to be the head, and give it the same class.

(c) Use what you know about the word *him* (as a noun phrase), and where it is likely to be found.

3.8 Adverb or degree modifier?

The following sentences include italicized adverbs which precede adjectives.

(44) *immensely* large

(45) *completely* impossible

(46) *totally* happy with his choice

(a) Show that the adverb is inside the adjective phrase.

(b) These adverbs function like degree modifiers such as *very*. Does this mean that the adverbs are actually degree modifiers here?

(c) Alternatively, does it mean that all the other degree modifiers are really adverbs?

3.9 ☞ *Enough*

What is unusual about the degree modifier *enough*?

3.10 Adjective phrases in other languages

For the corpus materials for Chinese, Madi and Tamil:

(a) Identify some adjective phrases.

(b) Work out which parts in the phrase correspond to adjective and degree modifier.

(c) What is the order of these parts in the phrase?

Look particularly at the following examples:

Chinese: D8, D9, J1, J2

Madi: D2 (compare with A5)

Tamil: D4, D8–10

3.11 Postpositions

Postposition

In some languages, prepositions come before a noun phrase, while in others they come *after* a noun phrase. A preposition which comes after a noun phrase is called a POSTPOSITION (you can still use the symbol P to stand for postposition, and PP for postposition phrase). Look at the corpus languages and work out which languages have prepositions and which have postpositions. Consider particularly the following sentences:

Chinese: F2, F4

Madi: F2

Malay: F5, F6

Tamil: F1, F2

THE VERB, THE VERB PHRASE AND THE AUXILIARIES

4

Verbs have distinctive word-shapes (morphologies). The verb heads a verb phrase. The verb can be preceded within the verb phrase by auxiliary and modal verbs, and the negation word *not*. The verb phrase is usually preceded by a noun phrase called the subject.

VERB

We have looked at four of the five major word classes: nouns, adjectives, adverbs and prepositions. It is time to introduce the fifth major word class: verbs. To understand what a VERB is, we need to think both about how it contributes to the meaning of the sentence as a whole, and also about the shape of the verb as a word, including its suffixes. A sentence represents an action or an event or a state of affairs In many cases, the verb is the word which names the kind of action or event or state of affairs. Thus in the sentence *I was reading the letter to John*, the verb *reading* names the kind of action involved. In contrast, noun phrases usually name the participants in the eventuality – the actors or things acted upon, such as *I* and *the letter* and *John*. The verb is a bit like the head of the sentence, both because it expresses the core meaning in some sense, and also because the most indispensable part of an English sentence is its verb. A command like *Eat!* is a sentence consisting just of a verb.

These considerations help us understand what a verb does, but the best way of actually identifying a verb is to look at its shape as a word. The shape of a word is its morphology, and this includes for example any suffixes or prefixes which are part of the word or can be added to the word, and any other changes which can be made to the shape of the word. English verbs have two distinctive morphological characteristics. The first special characteristic is that the shape of the verb can encode

Verb

the tense of the sentence; the sentence in (1) is present and the sentence in (2) is past, and this difference is coded by the morphology of the verb.

(1)   He eats meat.

(2)   He ate meat.

The second special morphological characteristic is that an English verb can agree with its subject if the verb is present and the subject is third person singular. (A third person singular form is a noun phrase such as *he* or *it* or *John*; it excludes plural noun phrases and noun phrases such as *I* or *you*.) AGREEMENT is a morphological change to a word which reflects the characteristics of some other word; in (3) the verb is morphologically changed by adding *-s* when the subject is third person singular. In (4) there is no morphological change to the verb because the subject is plural.

Agreement

(3)   He eats meat.

(4)   They eat meat.

Both tense and agreement are expressed only in the morphology of a verb. The sentence in (5) and the noun phrase in (6) describe roughly the same event, but (5) is a sentence containing a verb, as indicated by the fact that it carries tense, and (6) is a noun phrase containing a noun. A noun cannot morphologically express tense or agreement.

(5)   The building collapsed slowly yesterday.

(6)   the building's slow collapse which happened yesterday

In some old-style grammars, verbs are called 'doing words' and nouns are called 'naming words'. While these definitions fit the prototypical verbs and nouns, they do not work well when applied to (5) and (6), where the definitions do not differentiate *collapsed* and *collapse*. Instead, what clearly differentiates the verb from the noun is the morphology not the meaning.

VERB PHRASE

We have seen that a verb is a bit like the head of a sentence, but while there is some truth in this, it can be shown that a verb is really the head of a verb phrase which is contained within the sentence.

(7)

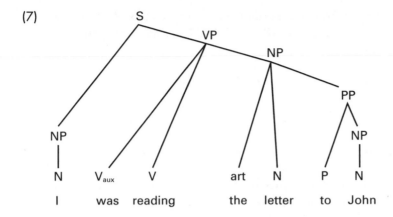

In this book I will make two crude assumptions (i) and (ii) about what is inside the verb phrase, along with the verb (which is its head), and suggest that you do the same, to simplify the drawing of tree structures. (For a more complex alternative, try Exercise 4.3).

(i)   The verb phrase contains anything which follows the verb within the same sentence.

(ii) The verb phrase contains the auxiliary verbs which precede the verb (i.e. words like *might, could, should, have, be* and *do*) and the negation word *not*.

Based on these assumptions, the only word in (7) which is not in the verb phrase is the word *I*, this being the noun phrase which precedes the verb. The verb phrase thus takes up most of the sentence.

What reasons are there for thinking that there is a verb phrase? First, there is some evidence from movement or deletion, accompanied by replacement (by *do*), which shows that the verb and the phrases which follow it stick together. The sentence in (8) shows both movement and replacement while the sentence in (9) shows deletion and replacement.

(8)   I said I would read the letter to John, and read the letter to John I did.

(9)   I said I would read the letter to John, and I did.

▶   **Is it possible to delete the verb phrase and NOT replace it with *did*? Why?**

Another piece of evidence for the verb phrase is that the verb and the phrases which follow it can stick together in an idiomatic expression; an IDIOM is a syntactic structure whose composite meaning is not **Idiom** predictable from the meaning of its parts Thus *threw* and *up* together are an idiom meaning vomit, and *kick* and *bucket* together are an idiom meaning die.

(10) John threw up. (can idiomatically mean John vomited)

(11) John kicked the bucket. (can idiomatically mean John died)

Note that the subject, the noun phrase *John* which is outside the verb phrase, is not part of the idiom. The boundaries of the idiom thus correspond to the boundaries of the verb phrase. There are no idioms such as (12) which include the subject and the verb but leave the object of the verb outside the idiom; such an idiom would violate the integrity of the verb phrase.

(12) The bucket fell on John. (can NOT idiomatically mean something killed John)

A third piece of evidence for the verb phrase comes from the various differences between a noun phrase which precedes the verb (called the subject) and a noun phrase which follows the verb (called the object). Consider examples (13)–(17).

In a sentence, the minimum requirement is a verb and, except in very special cases such as commands, a noun phrase preceding the verb. There need not be a noun phrase following the verb, and most verbs can be made to dispense with them. This is shown in sentences (14) and (15) below.

(13) The man ate the cheese.

(14) The man ate.

(15) The cheese was eaten.

In contrast, the noun phrase which precedes the verb cannot be dispensed with except in the very special kind of sentence seen in (17) which is a command (and has a kind of implicit subject *you*).

(16) *Ate the cheese.

(17) Eat the cheese!

The fact that the noun phrase following the verb can be dispensed with fits with the idea that the verb phrase contains the verb and this noun phrase; in all other kinds of phrase we have seen that all but the head can be dispensed with. In contrast, the fact that the noun phrase preceding the verb can NOT be dispensed with shows that it is not in the verb phrase (or it should, like everything else but the verb, be deletable).

GRAMMATICAL ROLES: SUBJECT AND OBJECT

In English, the sentence is made of a noun phrase and a verb phrase. This noun phrase is called the SUBJECT and in English is identifiable by position: in a declarative sentence (a sentence which makes a statement) it precedes the verb. The verb phrase is sometimes called the PREDICATE (note: this is not the same as the 'predicator' which is just the verb). The verb phrase contains a verb, which can be followed by a noun phrase which is called the OBJECT and is again identified by position (as the NP following the verb). If there is another NP following the object, it can be called second object. The terms subject and object are called grammatical roles, and are purely structural or formal notions in themselves unrelated to meaning. In some languages, grammatical roles are identified not by position but by the morphology of words in the phrase, a morphological characteristic called case. Thus for example in German, the subject is the noun phrase whose article is morphologically altered to express nominative case. Where case is used to identify grammatical roles, it is often possible for the order of phrases to be fairly free.

Subject

Predicate

Object

AUXILIARY VERBS AND MODALS

The noun word class is open because new nouns can be added to it, but it includes a subclass of nouns which is closed – the subclass of pronouns. Similarly, the verb word class is open, but it includes subclasses of verbs which are closed – the subclasses of auxiliary verbs and modal verbs. These two kinds of verb supplement the main verb which is the head of the verb phrase and expresses the kind of eventuality. They precede the main verb within the verb phrase and could be treated as rather like the closed class words (articles, and degree modifiers) which come at the beginning of other kinds of phrase. The only three auxiliary verbs – *be*, *have*, and *do* – are seen in (18)–(20).

(18) I am reading the book.

(19) I had read the book.

(20) I did read the book.

▶ **Find two kinds of evidence for the claim that the auxiliary verbs *be*, *have* and *do* as seen in (18)–(20) are verbs.**

English has a small group of modal verbs, which express possibility or necessity. Two of them are demonstrated in (21) and (22).

(21) I might read the book.

(22) I should read the book.

▶ **A sentence must have tense. How does this provide indirect evidence that the modals *might, should*, etc. are verbs?**

It is easy to distinguish the main verb from auxiliary or modal verbs. In English, the main verb is always the final (rightmost) verb in the sequence; if there is only one verb, it will almost always be the main verb. A complicating fact is that the words *do, have* and *be* exist both as auxiliary and as main verbs.

(23) I have eaten the cake.

(24) I have the cake.

▶ **Which of (23) and (24) uses the auxiliary verb *have* and which uses the main verb *have*?**

A sentence with modal and auxiliary verbs is illustrated in (25).

(25)

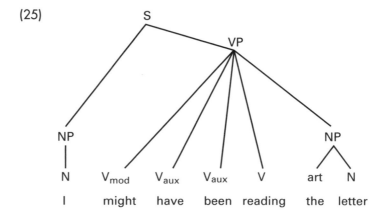

THE WORD *NOT*

We classify the word *not* in the following examples as in the word class **Negation** NEGATION. The word must appear immediately after an auxiliary verb or a modal verb. It can only appear after a main verb if the main verb is *be*, as in (30).

(26) I might not leave.

(27) I have not left.

(28) I did not leave.

(29) I am not leaving. (auxiliary verb *be* followed by main verb *leaving*)

(30) I am not happy. (main verb *be* followed by an adjective phrase *happy*)

(31) *I not left.

(32) *I left not.

A sample sentence with *not* in it is shown in (33).

(33)

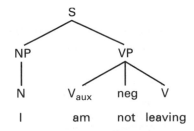

EXERCISES

4.1 Zero derivation

Two different words which sound the same are called HOMOPHONES. **Homophones**
It is possible for a noun to be changed into a verb which sounds the
same, so that the noun and verb are homophones. This process is
called ZERO-DERIVATION because no suffix or prefix is added. An **Zero-deviation**
example is the noun *table* which can be made into a verb and used in
the sentence *She tabled a motion*.

(a) Write out a list of twenty nouns.

(b) Which of these can be changed into verbs by zero-derivation?

(c) Can you formulate a generalization about which nouns can and
which nouns cannot?

4.2 Meaning and word class

The three sentences below all mean something rather similar, but the notion of thirst is expressed by three different word classes.

(34) She is thirsty for water.

(35) She has a thirst for water.

(36) She thirsts for water.

(a) Prove the word class of each word.

(b) Show how this provides evidence for the verb phrase as a constituent.

(c) Comment, using these sentences, on the traditional/schoolbook notion that a noun is a naming word, an adjective a describing word and a verb a doing word.

4.3 ☞ The V_{aux} and its phrase

If an auxiliary verb is a verb, then it should head a verb phrase. Make this assumption, and draw a new tree structure for the sentence in (7) *I was reading the letter to John*. Does this analysis have any advantages, or enable any insights?

4.4 ☞ A verb phrase as a modifier of a noun?

If the word *laughing* in the following example is a verb, why does this support the idea that there is a verb phrase?

(37) The laughing cavalier

4.5 ☞ Modality and word class

Modality   MODALITY is the expression of possibility (including permission) or necessity (including obligation). Modality can be expressed by a modal verb, or by a noun, adjective or adverb. Identify the modal verb, noun, adjective or adverb in the following examples.

(38) Is it really necessary to do this exercise?

(39) You might possibly know the answer to this.

(40) Modality is the expression of possibility.

4.6 The adverb phrase and the VP

Adverb phrases can roam free between the major phrases in a sentence, as illustrated in (41)–(45) with the modal adverb phrase *probably*. Why does the contribution of *probably* to the meaning of the sentence depend on where it is?

(41) Probably he was eating his dinner.

(42) He probably was eating his dinner.

(43) He was probably eating his dinner.

(44) He was eating probably his dinner.

(45) He was eating his dinner probably.

4.7 ☞ The word class of *never*

Does *never* belong to the word class negation (along with *not*) or the word class adverb? Answer this question by demonstrating the similarities or differences between *never* and *not*, and between *never* and any word which you know to be an adverb.

4.8 *didnae* and *didn't* (dialectal variation)

In some varieties of Scottish English, the word *didnae* is used, in a sentence like (46).

(46) He didnae do it.

On the surface this would seem to be the same word as the word *didn't* in a southern English sentence like (47).

(47) He didn't do it.

But we can see that there is a difference when we try to formulate a question in each of the dialects.

(48) Didn't he do it?

(49) * Didnae he do it?

(50) Did he no do it?

Speculate on what this tells us both about *didn't* and about *didnae*. What further sentences might you want to elicit from a speaker of this Scottish dialect in order to explore what is happening here?

5 THE SIMPLE SENTENCE AND ITS TREE STRUCTURE

This chapter shows you a set of strategies for drawing a tree structure for a sentence with one main verb. The problems of conjunction and compounds are also addressed.

THE COMPONENT PARTS OF A SENTENCE

Eventuality   A sentence represents an EVENTUALITY. An eventuality is an action or an event or a state of affairs: something that happens or something that is. The sentence represents an eventuality by separating out the type of eventuality from the abstract or concrete things which are involved in the eventuality. The type of the eventuality is prototypically represented by the verb, and the abstract or concrete things involved in the eventuality are prototypically represented by noun phrases. 'Prototypically' here implies that this is the usual case, but other word and phrase classes can do the same job.

> (1)   The man in the hat casually gave a slimy fish to Toby.

Here the eventuality type is an action of giving, represented by the verb *gave*. The things involved in the eventuality are represented by the three noun phrases, *the man in the hat* (the giver), *a slimy fish* (the thing given), and *Toby* (the thing given to). Apart from the type of eventuality and the things which participate in it, a part of the sentence can also express the circumstances of the eventuality. The adverb phrase *casually* expresses the circumstances here. The component parts of the sentence thus contribute distinct components of meaning to the overall meaning of the sentence.

HOW TO DRAW A TREE STRUCTURE FOR A SENTENCE

In this chapter you will learn how to turn your pieces of knowledge about phrase and sentence structure from the first few chapters into the ability to build a tree structure (2) for a sentence like (1)

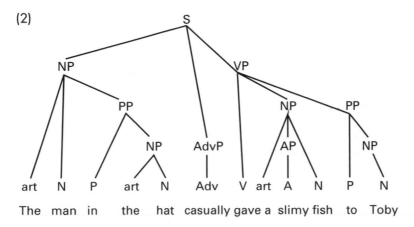

(2)

Here are some procedures for building the tree structure from the sentence. You can follow these steps in any order, or invent your own steps.

Step 1

Look for the main verb and write V above it.

We can see that the verb is *gave* because it is the word which carries tense, and only a verb can carry tense.

V

The man in the hat casually gave a slimy fish to Toby

Step 2

A verb is always inside a verb phrase, so draw a line up from V to VP.

The man in the hat casually gave a slimy fish to Toby

Step 3

A verb phrase is usually inside a sentence, so draw a line up from VP to S. S is the root of the tree, the node which contains everything else.

Almost every rule has to be hedged by adding 'usually' in this way: you should learn the usual case but be aware of special cases.

The man in the hat casually gave a slimy fish to Toby

Step 4

Now identify the noun phrases by the substitution test. A noun phrase might be replaceable by *he* or *she* or *it*. In this sentence, *the man in the hat* is replaceable by *he*, *a slimy fish* is replaceable by *it*, and *Toby* is replaceable by *him*, so here are three noun phrases.

The man in the hat casually gave a slimy fish to Toby

He   casually gave it   to him

Step 5

Underline the NPs and write NP above each of them.

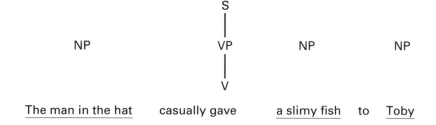

Step 6

Identify any articles in the sentence (*the* or *a* or *an*), and write art above them.

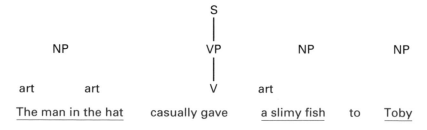

Step 7

Identify any nouns in the sentence, and write N above them. You know that nouns can often be pluralized and this is true of *man, hat* and *fish*. And you know that names are nouns, so *Toby* is a noun.

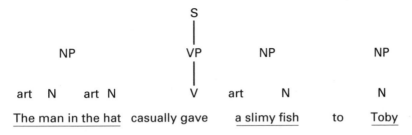

Step 8

An article is always immediately under NP, and N is always immediately under NP. If we work from right to left, we can start by drawing some lines up:

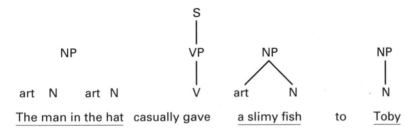

But what do we do about the fact that at the beginning of the sentence we have two separate sequences of Art N, but so far have identified only one NP for them to fit into? We cannot put them both into the same NP; each pair must be in its own NP, so we add another NP node and draw the lines like this:

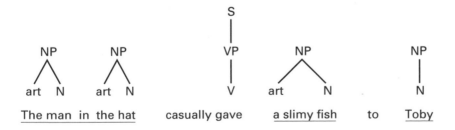

There is something wrong here because we know that [*the man in the hat*] is a single noun phrase, not two side by side, but we will fix it in a moment.

Step 9

The next stage is to identify the prepositions. If you aren't initially sure how to do this, the best thing is just to learn a list of common prepositions, which includes *in* and *to*. Write P above the prepositions.

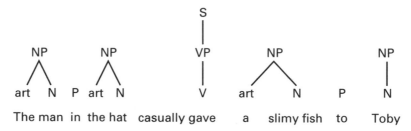

Step 10

A preposition is always in a preposition phrase, so write PP above each preposition and join it up.

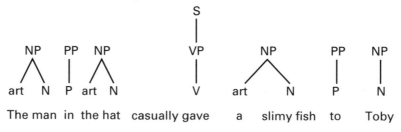

Step 11

Now let's start putting things together. This will involve some redrawing of the sentence, because we need to put some of the phrases inside other phrases; they are not all just next to each other. We will proceed from right to left, across the sentence. This is generally quite a good way to proceed when drawing tree structures. The first thing is to put the NP *Toby* in the PP with *to*; we know that *to Toby* is a single phrase because we can move it. It is also generally the case that a preposition is followed by a noun phrase, with the two together forming a PP.

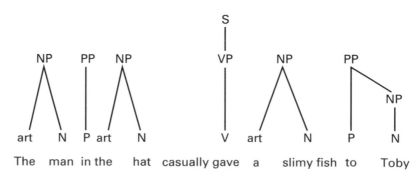

Now we put the two phrases which follow the verb into the verb phrase, with the verb, on the general assumption that material which follows the verb in the same sentence is inside the verb phrase. As always, this assumption is not always guaranteed to be correct.

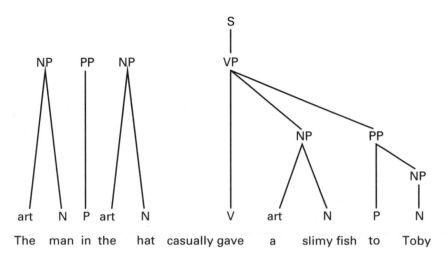

We know that a preposition is usually followed by a noun phrase, with the two together forming a preposition phrase, and so we can put the NP *the hat* into the PP with *in*.

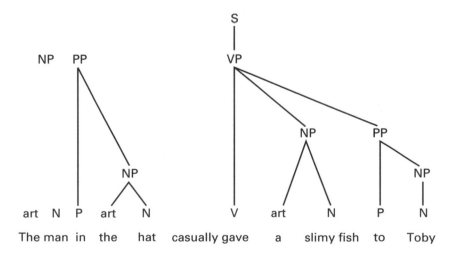

And we know that [*the man in the hat*] is all a single noun phrase because it can be replaced by *he*, and so we put the PP *in the hat* as a co-constituent with *man*:

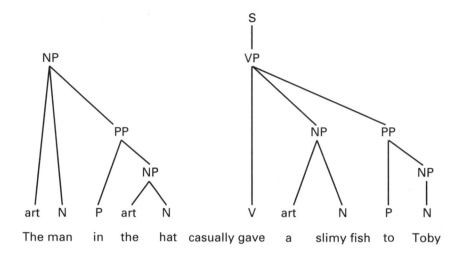

Finally, we draw a line from NP to S; this noun phrase which is the subject precedes the verb and so is directly in the sentence.

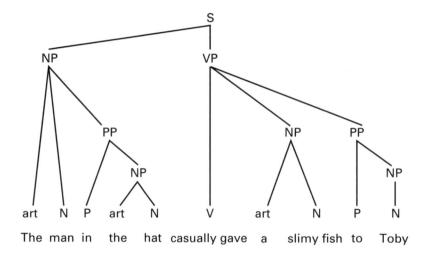

What we've just done is to work out which phrases belong inside which other phrases. We used the tests for phrase structure of movement and replacement to find out the phrase structures, along with our knowledge of stereotypical phrase structures.

Step 12

We haven't quite finished, because we have two words which are not yet part of the tree. These words *casually* and *slimy* pass the morphological tests for both adjectives and adverbs because they can both be made comparative, and can both have *very* put in front of them. However, we can tell that *casually* is an adverb, partly because it ends in *-ly* as many adverbs do, and mainly because it can roam free inside the sentence.

> Casually, the man in the hat gave a slimy fish to Toby.
> The man in the hat casually gave a slimy fish to Toby.
> The man in the hat gave a slimy fish casually to Toby.
> The man in the hat gave a slimy fish to Toby casually.

Thus we can identify *casually* as an adverb, mark it as such and put it in an adverb phrase, and then straight into the sentence.

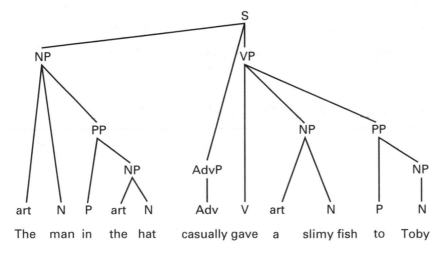

Note that *casually* is not part of the preceding noun phrase. First of all, adverbs do not directly appear inside noun phrases. Second, we know that *casually* can be moved on its own, independently of the noun phrase. And third, we can substitute the noun phrase by *he* while leaving *casually* untouched.

Step 13

The final step is to identify *slimy*. The tests tell us it is an adjective or an adverb, but since it is clearly inside the noun phrase because it is preceded by an article and followed by a noun, it must be an adjective in an adjective phrase. Its morphology incidentally also tells us that it is an adjective made by adding *-y* to the noun *slime*.

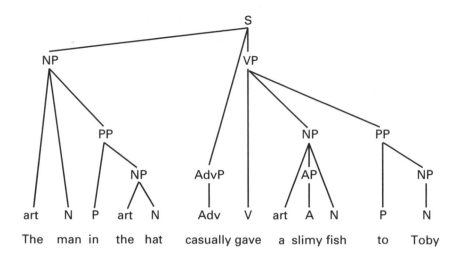

SUMMARY: WORKING OUT A TREE STRUCTURE

Here are some of the principles and rules we followed in working out the tree structure.

- Identify the verb first, using the tense test if necessary.
- Next identify the noun phrases, using substitution by a pronoun and any other appropriate tests. Once you have identified verb and noun phrases, you have a good sense of the overall shape of the sentence.
- Assume that every noun, verb, adjective, adverb and preposition is in its own phrase. So if you have two nouns you have two noun phrases, though one might be inside another, as we saw.
- If you find a preposition, look to see whether it combines with the following NP to form a PP.
- Once you have a PP, look to see whether it combines with the preceding noun to form a larger NP. In the sentence we looked at, one of the PPs does this and the other does not.
- An article is always in its own NP, and is usually at the beginning of it.
- An adverb (phrase) can usually be moved freely throughout the sentence. It rarely appears directly inside a noun phrase.
- Work from right to left across the sentence. This isn't a strict rule, but I think it makes the task easier.
- Remember that tests don't always work. Substitution by a pronoun did not identify *the hat* as a noun phrase, and instead we identified it as a noun phrase by the fact that it contains an article and a noun.

You might want to double-check the tree structure once you have drawn it. Try various substitution and movement tests on the phrases you have identified. Some phrases resist these tests, but there should usually be some supplementary evidence to show that you are on the right track.

Finally, make sure that in your tree structure it is always clear which node is under which other node; there should be no horizontal lines connecting nodes. And there should be no crossing lines.

HOW TO DESCRIBE A TREE STRUCTURE

The tree structure is made of labelled nodes and lines which connect those nodes. Labelled nodes in this tree include the nodes V, VP, S, art, NP, etc. Every node is labelled. Every node is connected by a line to at least one other node. The lines indicate containment: a node is contained in another node, or contains another node.

Containment can be immediate or non-immediate. The VP immediately contains an NP. The VP non-immediately contains an N, because the N is contained in the NP which is contained in the VP. The nodes which are contained are called constituents, and thus there are immediate constituents and non-immediate constituents. The topmost node is S, and is called the root of the tree; it contains immediately or non-immediately all the other nodes.

Where one node contains another, the containing node is called the mother and the contained node is the daughter. Where a mother node contains several daughters, the daughters are said to be sisters to each other.

THE PROBLEM OF CONJUNCTION

CONJUNCTION (also called coordination) is the joining of two constituents, usually of the same kind, to make a larger constitituent of the same kind and level. So two NPs are joined to make a larger NP. Conjunction involves the coordinating conjunctions *and* and *or*.

Conjunction

(3)   The man and the woman are leaving now.

(4)

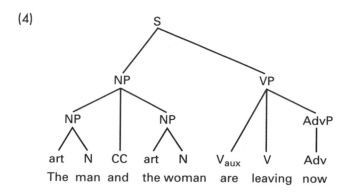

▶ **How do we know that *The man and the woman* form a single noun phrase?**

Conjoined structures break a general rule of phrase structure because the phrase containing the conjuncts does not have a head. Instead the phrase just contains two kinds of phrase of the same kind. It is also possible to conjoin words as in (5), where *old* is understood to apply to both *man* and *woman*.

(5) The old man and woman are leaving now.

(6)

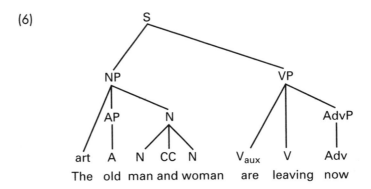

COMPOUND WORDS

Compound A compound word, usually called just a COMPOUND, is a combination of words into a single word. In English the internal structure of compounds falls outside the domain of syntax. Some compounds are listed in (7). Note that they are written sometimes as a single word, sometimes as two, and sometimes with a hyphen between them.

(7) Headroom, living room, boxcar, table lamp, queen bee, blackbird, greenhouse, blackboard, whitecap, redcap, sad-sack, meat-eating, window-cleaning, head-scratching, body-builder, meat-eater, hip-hugger, thief-taker.

Compounds are unalterable in a way that phrasal structures are not. One of the words cannot just be omitted or replaced or moved; they are frozen, and hence clearly distinguishable from phrasal structures. In syntax, each component part tends to add meaning in a clearly predictable way to the whole. In most though not all compounds the relation between the meaning of the parts and the whole is not predictable in the same way; for example, a female blackbird (*blackbird* as compound) is a brown bird not a black bird. When you come across one, treat it as in (8) as a single word with a single category, even if – as is usually the case – you can see other words inside it; these other words are syntactically irrelevant.

(8)

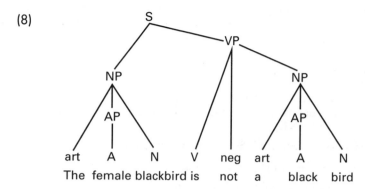

art A N V neg art A N
The female blackbird is not a black bird

EXERCISES

5.1 ☞ Nodes in a tree

Here is a tree structure for a sentence. It has nineteen nodes. In this exercise we do not count the words themselves as nodes, but we do count the category labels for the words as nodes.

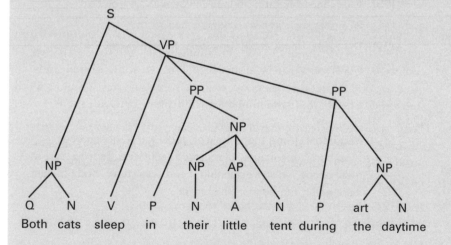

Q N V P N A N P art N
Both cats sleep in their little tent during the daytime

(a) How many root nodes does it have?

(b) What are the sisters of the VP node?

(c) How many daughters does the VP node have?

(d) How many immediate constituent nodes does the VP node have?

(e) How many immediate and non-immediate constituent nodes does the VP node have?

(f) How many NPs does each P have as sisters?

5.2 ☞ Practice tree structures for sentences

Draw tree structures for these sentences.

(9)   Peter slept.

(10) He probably left the city on Wednesday.

(11) The men on the train gave us tickets.

(12) The dogs were attacking the snake.

(13) The cats eat breakfast really slowly.

(14) The men with beards walked across the garden without shoes.

(15) The roads in the city gradually deteriorated over time.

(16) The women got really angry at the behaviour.

(17) I gave Mary the quite expensive book reluctantly.

(18) We deliberately made him a richer person.

(19) She almost sold the books to them for a pound.

(20) The plane took off from the runway without trouble.

(21) Probably she did not recognize their faces.

(22) The broken ones could have been thrown away.

(23) It is snowing lightly.

5.3 Tree structures for structural ambiguities

Draw two alternative tree structures for each of these sentences from Chapter 1 Exercise 1.1. You should find that the alternative depends on whether a PP is part of the noun phrase with the preceding noun, or not.

(24) Peter untied the parcel for Toby.

(25) Kes pushed the ping-pong ball under the sofa.

(26) I drove the visitor from Glasgow.

5.4 Coordination

(a) Make up:

(i)   a sentence with two coordinated verb phrases

(ii)   a sentence with two coordinated noun phrases

(iii)   a sentence with two coordinated adjective phrases

(iv)   a sentence with two coordinated adverb phrases

(v)   a sentence with two coordinated preposition phrases

(vi)   a sentence with two coordinated verbs

(vii)   a sentence with two coordinated nouns

(viii) a sentence with two coordinated adjectives

(ix)   a sentence with two coordinated adverbs

(x)   a sentence with two coordinated prepositions

(b)   Some closed class words can be coordinated; others cannot. Give examples for each closed class which can be coordinated.

(c)   List the closed class words which cannot be coordinated.

5.5 ☞ Compounds whose internal structure resembles phrases

In some compounds, the relation between the parts of the compound is similar to the relation between the parts of a phrase. Look at the compounds listed in (7) and identify compounds for which this is true. Can you formulate any generalizations?

5.6   Names

Names can consist of several words, sometimes also preceded by respect titles, such as *Napoleon Bonaparte* or *Mr John Smith* or *President Clinton* or *King James the sixth of Scotland*. Are these names compounds or phrases?

5.7   Coordination in other languages

Draw tree structures for the following sentences which illustrate coordination in the languages of the corpus. For Madi and Tamil in particular you will have to decide how to draw tree structures for coordination structures unlike English.

Chinese: K1

Madi: K1, K2

Malay: K1, K2

Tamil: K1, K2

5.8 Negation, auxiliary and modals in other languages

For each language in the corpus describe the order and position in the sentence of: negation, auxiliary and modal verbs and the main verb. You do not need to restrict yourself to looking at sections G and H, though these are the most relevant.

5.9 Sentence structure trees in other languages

Draw tree structures for the following simple sentences from the corpus. Continue to add word-for-word translations under the sentences in the corpus as you do so.

Chinese: A1, B1, D8, H1

Madi: A1, A5, D2, F1, H1 (Note: you will have to make a decision on the word class of *ra*; make a best guess if you have to. If you are unsure about *not*, look at M1 in comparison with H2.)

Malay: A1, D1, D10, F6, H3 (Note: you will have to decide what *telah* is; try comparing the B sentences with each other.)

Tamil: A1, D8, F1, H1

5.10 The order of grammatical words in other languages

For each language in the corpus, work out the order of grammatical words, head and other phrases in:

(a) the sentence (here, you may find that order is not fixed, or is only partly fixed);

(b) the adjective phrase;

(c) the noun phrase;

(d) the preposition phrase.

Now, for each language find out whether there is any consistency of order between the different kinds of phrase and the sentence.
 For example, this is what you might do with Chinese:

(a) *the sentence appears to have a basic subject – auxiliary – verb – object order (S V_{aux} V O), illustrated, for example, by G3.*

(b) the adjective phrase has an order deg – A, illustrated by D8.

 On the basis of just these two, we could say that there seems to be a consistent ordering of closed class word before the head (as in English, in fact). In order to complete this analysis of Chinese we would now look at noun phrase and preposition phrase.

NOUN PHRASES

6

Noun phrases can have various constituents at their beginning, including genitive noun phrases, demonstrative, article, quantifier and numeral. Noun phrases can also contain sentences, called relative clauses.

WHAT YOU ALREADY KNOW ABOUT NOUN PHRASES

We have so far seen just three types of position for a noun phrase:

- The noun phrase is found as a daughter of S, preceding the verb phrase; this noun phrase is called the subject.
- The noun phrase is found as a daughter of VP, following the verb. The noun phrase which immediately follows the verb is called the object. Two or more noun phrases can appear after the verb, in which case they can be called first object, second object and so on.
- The noun phrase is found as a daughter of PP, following the preposition.

A noun phrase is not found in English as a daughter of AP or as a daughter of AdvP. As regards its internal structure, we know that the noun phrase can begin with an article, followed by an adjective phrase, followed by the noun, followed by a preposition phrase.

The best test for a noun phrase is that it can be replaced by a pronoun. Noun phrases can often also be moved, and can sometimes be omitted.

A NOUN PHRASE CAN APPEAR AT THE BEGINNING OF ANOTHER NOUN PHRASE

We can now add to our comments about both the distribution and the internal structure of noun phrases, by showing that a noun phrase can appear directly inside another noun phrase.

(1)   I read the man's book.

(2)   I read the old man's book.

(3)   I read John's book.

(4)   I read his book.

▶   **Identify the noun phrases in the above sentences.**

Each of the noun phrases following *read* in these examples has as its first (leftmost) constituent another noun phrase. We can tell that these are noun phrases not only because they clearly have the internal structure of noun phrases (*The man's* begins with an article and contains a noun) but also because they can be substituted by a pronoun (*The man's* can be substituted by *his*). So the tree structure for (1) is:

(5)

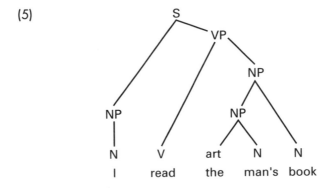

Genitive   This noun phrase at the beginning of another noun phrase is sometimes called a GENITIVE NP, or an NP in the genitive case. It can often express possession, as in the above sentences.

CLOSED CLASS WORDS CAN APPEAR AT THE BEGINNING OF A NOUN PHRASE

We know that the word *the* or *a* or *an* can appear at the beginning of a noun phrase, and that these words belong to a closed class. We now see some more types of closed class word which also appear at the beginning of a noun phrase. One such class of word is DEMONSTRATIVE. In most dialects of English there are four demonstratives: *this, that, these* and *those*. In some dialects of English there are others, such as *yon*.

Demonstrative

(6)

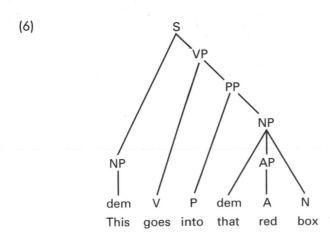

As this example shows, demonstratives differ from articles in that demonstratives can optionally be left on their own inside the noun phrase, without a noun. This is the first example we have seen of a noun phrase which does not contain a noun. Because the noun phrase lacks the noun which should be its head, we say that this noun phrase is a HEADLESS PHRASE.

Headless phrase

Another closed class of word which can appear at the beginning of a noun phrase is the QUANTIFIER. A few examples of quantifiers are: *every, each, some, all, no*.

Quantifier

(7)

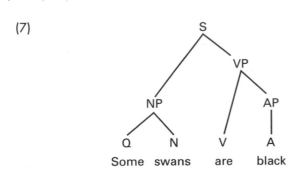

numeral   Finally, a NUMERAL can also come at the beginning of a noun phrase. A numeral is a word such as *five* or *fifty* or a phrase such as *a thousand*.

(8)

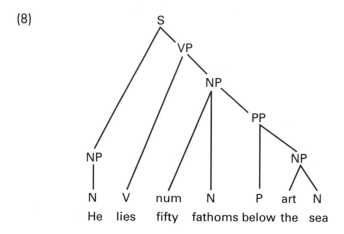

He lies fifty fathoms below the sea

Words of the classes article, demonstrative, quantifier and numeral appear at the beginning of the noun phrase. Since they are closed class words and hence easy to recognize, this provides another useful diagnostic for discovering noun phrases in a sentence.

PARTITIVES

Partitive   We have seen that a noun phrase can be headless when it does not immediately contain a noun. This makes possible a certain kind of structure called a PARTITIVE, which begins with a quantifier or numeral or other closed class word, has no head noun, and is followed by a PP. It is illustrated in (9).

(9)

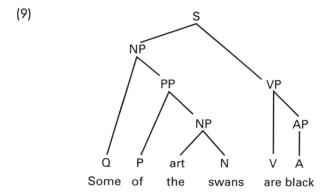

Some of the swans are black

This is fairly counter-intuitive; just by looking at the meaning it would seem at first as though *swans* was the head of [*Some of the swans*], just as *swans* is the head of [*Some swans*]. However, one way of thinking of partitives is that they have an invisible word such as *instances* or *ones* as their head; so *some of the swans* can be thought of as *some ones of the swans* or *some instances of the swans*.

RELATIVE CLAUSES

A noun phrase can contain a sentence which is called a RELATIVE CLAUSE. An example is given in (10).

Relative clause

> (10) I read *the book* <u>which you gave to me</u>.

The overall sentence (called the root sentence) contains two verbs – *read* and *gave*. If there are two verbs, there are two verb phrases, and hence two sentences, one ultimately contained inside the other. The contained sentence – the relative clause – is [*which you gave to me*].

▶ **Apply the usual tests for noun phrase to show that [*which you gave to me*] is inside a noun phrase [*the book which you gave to me*].**

The structure for this noun phrase is fairly straightforward: the clause is an S inside the NP, as in (11).

(11)

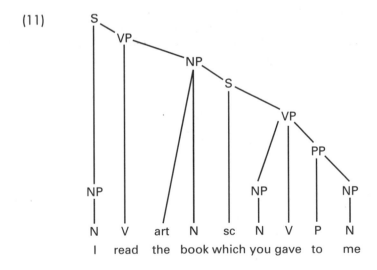

The one new class of word we see here involves the word *which* at the beginning of the relative clause, which we call a RELATIVE PRONOUN. Some more examples of sentences containing noun phrases (italicized) which in turn contain relative clauses (underlined) are given below.

Relative pronoun

(12) *The man <u>who you met</u> is my brother.*

(13) *The ceiling <u>that fell down</u> is the one in the bathroom.*

(14) This is *the place <u>where it all fell in</u>.*

EXERCISES

6.1 ☞ Practice tree structures for NP containing a genitive NP

(a) Identify the noun phrases in the following sentences (e.g. using pronoun substitution).

(b) Draw a tree structure for each sentence.

(c) For each genitive NP such as *Mary's* or *the terrified crow's*, describe its relation to the noun: i.e. is it possessive, or something else?

  (15) She is Mary's cat.
  (16) We ignored the terrified crow's screech.
  (17) It was simply my opinion.
  (18) The building's capture was inevitable.

6.2 ☞ The location of genitive *-s*

The suffix *-s* is used to make a noun phrase genitive and so permit it to come at the beginning of (and inside) another noun phrase. Does this suffix always attach to the noun in the noun phrase or does it just come after the last word in the noun phrase, whether or not it is a noun? Consider these examples and add some of your own.

  (19) She was the man we met's sister.
  (20) It was the boy on the train's fault.

6.3 *It's* as an error

Here are two alternative ways of writing the word *its*. (21) is a very common punctuation mistake.

  (21) It's wing is broken.
  (22) Its wing is broken.

(a) What reasonable grounds are there for thinking that (21) is the wrong way to write this word?

(b)   Why nevertheless do many people write the word like this? Don't
just assume ignorance; such a widespread practice is likely to
some have rationale.

6.4   ☞ Dialectal variation: *them books*

(23) I saw those books yesterday.

(24) I saw them books yesterday.

(25) I saw they books yesterday.

(26) I saw that books yesterday.

These sentences illustrate grammatical sentences in different dialects of
English. Of these, the first is the standard dialect. What is the simplest
way of explaining how the other dialects differ from this standard?

6.5   Are demonstratives a distinct class?

What we are calling demonstratives are sometimes called either adjectives or pronouns in other grammatical descriptions of English. What
evidence is there for or against either of these different ways of labelling
the words *this, that, these* and *those*?

6.6   ☞ Headless noun phrases

Which of the following kinds of noun phrase can be headless?

An NP beginning with an article (try this with and without an adjective phrase such as *poorest*)

An NP beginning with a genitive NP

An NP beginning with a demonstrative

An NP beginning with a quantifier (try different quantifiers)

An NP beginning with a numeral

6.7   Tree structures for NPs

Draw tree structures for the following sentences, which contain some
complex or difficult NPs.

(27) Two of us are not happy.

(28) She gave her all.

(29) They were in such a mess.

(30) Several days previously the parcel had arrived.

(31) It was at the very bottom.

6.8 ☞ The beginning of the NP (order)

The following noun phrases show various possible sequences at the beginning of a noun phrase.

(a)　Draw a tree structure for each noun phrase.

(b)　List the possible combinations of article, demonstrative, numeral, quantifier and genitive NP. For example, (32) shows a sequence of genitive + numeral + noun.

(c)　Are any logically possible sequences actually ungrammatical?

(32)　John's five books

(33)　every two minutes

(34)　his every word

(35)　the two men

(36)　the many people who came

(37)　all the words

(38)　all John's words

(39)　all those pictures

(40)　those many speeches

6.9 *None*

What class of word is *none*? In order to decide, invent several sentences with *none* in them and draw tree structures for them.

6.10 ☞ *Their finally acknowledging their mistake*

(41)　*Their finally acknowledging their mistake* is a great relief.

(a)　What is the phrase class of the italicized constituent in this sentence?

(b)　Draw a tree structure for this phrase.

(c)　Why does this present a problem for the theory that the verb is in a verb phrase which excludes the subject of the sentence?

6.11 ☞ Relative clauses

(a)　Here are some sentences containing noun phrases with relative clauses (relative clauses underlined) in English. Draw a tree structure for each whole sentence, which includes a tree structure also for the relative clause.

(42) A person <u>who I spoke to</u> gave me directions.

(43) Everyone <u>that I met</u> was very helpful

(44) The bird <u>I saw</u> had yellow feet.

(45) I found someone <u>to leave my fortune to</u>.

(b) Now draw a tree structure for the following sentence. You will need to decide what to do about the constituent *who I spoke to*. For example, is it a relative clause?

(46) Who I spoke to is none of your business.

6.12 Complex noun phrases in other languages

Draw tree structures for the following sentences from the corpus, all of which contain noun phrases, some quite complex. If you think any of the words belong to new classes, invent class names for them.

Chinese: B1, D9

Madi: A7, D4, E1

Malay: D3, D4, D8

Tamil: D4, D7, E2

7 ROOT SENTENCE AND SUBORDINATE CLAUSES

> Subordinate clauses are sentences which are contained inside a larger sentence or inside a phrase. The topmost or overall sentence which contains everything else, including any subordinate clauses, is called the root sentence. Root sentence and subordinate clause are both kinds of sentence, but differ in some respects.

ROOT SENTENCE AND SUBORDINATE CLAUSE

Recursion We have seen that it is possible to put a sentence inside a noun phrase, which in turn is inside a sentence. This is an example of RECURSION, where a thing is put directly or indirectly inside something else of the same kind. The fact that languages are recursive means that there is no upper limit on the length of a sentence. The following nursery rhyme stanza is all one sentence, exploiting the possibility of putting a clause inside a noun phrase inside a clause inside a noun phrase and so on. It could be added to indefinitely.

> (1)
> This is the farmer sowing his corn
> that kept the cock that crowed in the morn
> that waked the priest all shaven and shorn
> that married the man all tattered and torn
> that kissed the maiden all forlorn
> that milked the cow with the crumpled horn
> that tossed the dog
> that worried the cat
> that killed the rat
> that ate the malt
> that lay in the house that Jack built.

In a tree structure there is a single topmost node, which we call the root node, the node from which the rest of the tree grows downwards. This topmost node is S, and so the sentence as a whole which is symbolized by this root S is called the ROOT SENTENCE. Most other sentences which are contained directly or indirectly inside this root sentence are called SUBORDINATE CLAUSES; we could call them subordinate sentences but by calling them clauses instead of sentences we draw attention to some differences between the root and the subordinate versions of sentences. The relative clauses which we saw at the end of the previous chapter are examples of subordinate clauses as modifiers of a noun inside a noun phrase. Here are some examples of root sentences which contain subordinate clauses; the subordinate clauses in each case are underlined.

Root sentence

Subordinate clauses

(2) I said <u>I was leaving</u>.

(3) <u>Whether he has gone</u> is a mystery.

(4) We told him <u>that it looked pointless</u>.

(5) We ate <u>where we ate yesterday</u>.

(6) <u>Because he left</u> we sighed with relief.

(7) The belief <u>that the earth is flat</u> is a widespread belief.

(8) She is happy <u>to join us</u>.

(9) Soon after <u>I left</u>, the party ended.

▶ **Use movement, substitution and other tests for the sentences in (2)–(9) to confirm for each subordinate clause what kind of constituent it is inside.**

We know that these root sentences contain a subordinate clause because all of them have two verbs; each verb must be in a sentence of its own, hence one verb is in the root sentence and the second verb is in a subordinate sentence (clause). Some of these subordinate clauses are contained directly under S, while others are in VP, or NP, or AP or PP. An example of each is shown in the tree structures below.

(10)

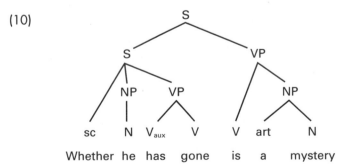

(11)

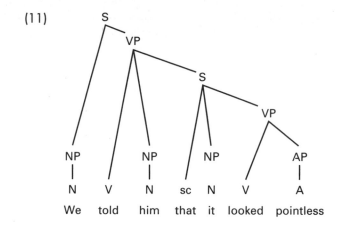

(12)

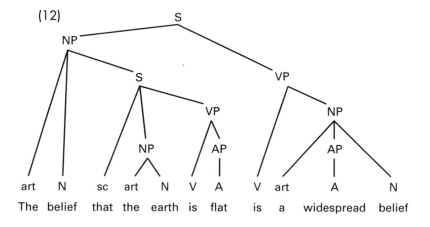

(13)

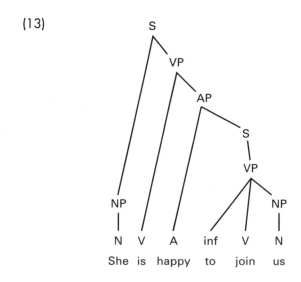

(14)

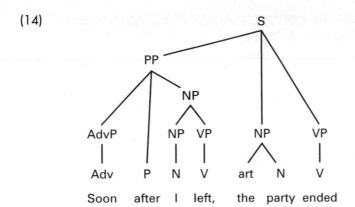

Soon after I left, the party ended

COORDINATION OF ROOT SENTENCES AND SUBORDINATE CLAUSES

Coordination breaks the normal rules of structure, because it takes two or more constituents of a certain type and joins them to form a larger constituent of the same type and level. It is thus possible for coordination to take two root sentences and join them to form a single larger root sentence.

(15)

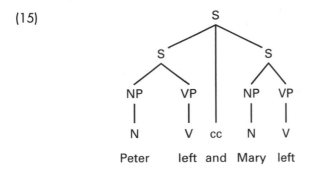

Peter left and Mary left

If two root sentences are related by being conjoined, then it should in principle be possible to change the order as in the following examples. The fact that the meaning of (17) is peculiar is not an effect relating to sentence structure but relates to how a discourse sequence of root sentences is generally understood as expressing sequence in time.

(16) He jumped and he broke his leg.

(17) He broke his leg and he jumped.

DIFFERENCES BETWEEN A ROOT SENTENCE AND SUBORDINATE CLAUSE

In English, there are several structural differences between a root sentence and a subordinate clause, which can help identify subordinate clauses when drawing a tree structure.

(i) A subordinate clause can start with a characteristic subordinating word. One example of this is the relative pronoun at the beginning of a noun phrase. Other subordinating words belong to the class of **Subordinating conjunctions** SUBORDINATING CONJUNCTIONS, also called complementizers: *that, whether, because, if* and *how* are some of them. Subordinating conjunctions come only at the beginning of a subordinate clause, which makes them a good clue. In the following examples, the subordinate clause is underlined, and the subordinating word is in boldface.

(18) I left **because** I wanted to catch the train.

(19) I asked **whether** John was leaving.

(20) I said **that** he was leaving.

(21)

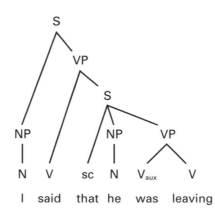

(ii) A subordinate clause can also start with a subordinating phrase, often a question phrase. Here are some examples.

(22) When we arrived the party began.

(23) How difficult this is going to be depends on you.

(24) I asked <u>whose book this is</u>.

(25)

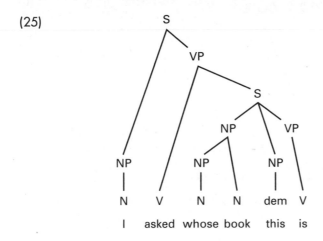

Root sentences can also begin with question phrases like this, but with various differences.

▶ **What is the difference between (24) and the root sentence** *Whose book is this?*

(iii)   The verb in a subordinate clause can be preceded by the infinitive marker *to*. This word sounds the same as (is a homophone with) the preposition *to* but it is not actually a preposition here. We call it 'inf' when we draw a tree structure, and assume that it relates in some way to the expression of tense, putting it in the verb phrase (like an auxiliary). The verb in a root clause cannot be preceded by *to*.

(26) I wanted <u>to leave</u>.

(27)

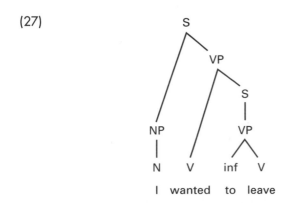

Where the verb is preceded by *to* it is possible for the subordinate clause as a whole to begin with the subordinating conjunction *for*.

(28) I wanted very much <u>for John to leave</u>.

(29)

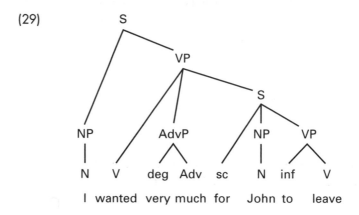

(iv)   The subject noun phrase (the noun phrase which precedes the verb) in a subordinate clause can be in the ACCUSATIVE case. This is visible only if the subject is a pronoun, where instead of for example *I* we can have the accusative *me*; similarly *us* or *him* or *her* or *them* are distinctive accusative forms.

Accusative

(30) He wanted <u>me to leave</u>.

(31)

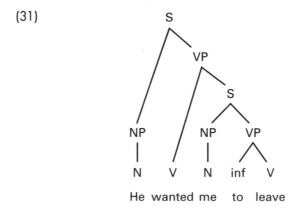

The subject of a root clause cannot be accusative; if we make up a root sentence with *me* as the subject, it will be ungrammatical.

(32) * Me wanted to leave.

(v)   Finally, it is worth remembering that a subordinate clause is a constituent, and has the characteristics of a constituent. Like a noun phrase, it can be the subject of a sentence, the object of the verb; and it can be a modifier – like an adverb phrase or a preposition phrase. It can be moved, replaced, and deleted like a constituent. If it is inside another constituent then whatever happens to the larger constituent will affect the subordinate clause. Like other kinds of constituent, the subordinate clause has a characteristic meaning which is similar to that of a root sentence: the subordinate clause is itself usually a statement about the world, representing an eventuality (or a question about an eventuality). The verbs which take subordinate clauses as objects are often verbs such as *say*, which take statements about the world as objects.

HOW TO DRAW A TREE STRUCTURE FOR A SENTENCE WITH TWO MAIN VERBS

Where a root sentence contains two verbs, then one verb is the root verb, the verb whose VP is directly contained in the root sentence. The other verb is a subordinate verb, a verb whose VP is contained in a subordinate clause inside the root sentence. In practical terms, drawing a tree structure for such a sentence means identifying which verb is subordinate and then working out which other words and phrases belong to the subordinate clause, with the subordinate clause then treated as a phrase within the larger sentence. Various approaches are possible, drawing on the distinctive characteristics of subordinate clauses just discussed, or using tests for constituent structure (replacement, movement, deletion) to identify the subordinate clause as a constituent.

Here, then, are some suggestions, illustrated with examples. In the examples, the underlined material is the subordinate clause.

(i)   If a verb is preceded by *to*, it is in a subordinate clause.

(33) They asked <u>to be shown the best table</u>.

(ii)   If the subject of the verb is in so-called accusative case; that is, if it is one of the pronouns *me, him, her, us* or *them*, then the clause is subordinate (see Exercise 7.3 for a complication).

(34) They wanted <u>me to read them the book</u>.

(iii)   If there is a subordinating conjunction, then it is at the beginning of a subordinate clause (e.g. the main verb which follows it is subordinate).

(35) They thought <u>that I should be there</u>.

(36) <u>Whether I was or was not there </u>was immaterial.

(iv)   A subordinate clause within an NP (i.e. a relative clause) will be replaced along with the rest of the NP by substituting the whole constituent with the word *it*. Subordinate clauses within other kinds of phrase can similarly be replaced along with the rest of the phrase.

(37)   The bird <u>that was ruthlessly hunted</u> has become extinct.

(38)   It   has become extinct.

(39)   They were very proud <u>that he was accepted</u>.

(40)   They were   proud.

(v)   A subordinate clause within a phrase will be moved along with the rest of the phrase. Note that the subordinate clause in the following sentence has none of the other characteristics; we know it is subordinate because movement shows us that it is contained in the NP.

(41)   He answered the question <u>I asked</u>.

(42)   The question <u>I asked</u> was answered by him.

(vi)   A subordinate clause can sometimes roam free within a larger sentence or VP, like an adverb phrase. Such subordinate clauses will usually begin with a subordinating conjunction.

(43)   <u>Because we were late</u> they decided to start eating.

(44)   They decided <u>because we were late</u> to start eating.

(45)   They decided to start eating <u>because we were late</u>.

(vii)   A subordinate clause can sometimes be moved to the beginning or end of the sentence.

(46)   I don't know <u>whether this will help</u>.

(47)   <u>Whether this will help</u>, I don't know.

(viii)   A subordinate clause can sometimes be replaced by *it*, or by a demonstrative such as *this* or *that*. This shows that there is a similarity between subordinate clause and noun phrase.

(48)   She told me <u>that she was leaving</u>.

(49) She told me this.

(ix) A subordinate clause can sometimes be questioned, replaced with *what* or some similar word or phrase. Often *what* will also be moved to the beginning of the sentence.

(50) She told me what?

(51) <u>What did she tell me?</u>

HOW TO DRAW A TREE STRUCTURE FOR A SENTENCE WITH THREE OR MORE MAIN VERBS

If there are two main verbs within the same root sentence, one will be root and the other subordinate. Where there are three main verbs, there are two subordinate verbs, each in its own sentence. The two subordinate sentences could be connected; one could be inside the other as in (52) or they might be unconnected as in (54).

(52) I said <u>that Mary told me </u>that she was leaving.

(53)

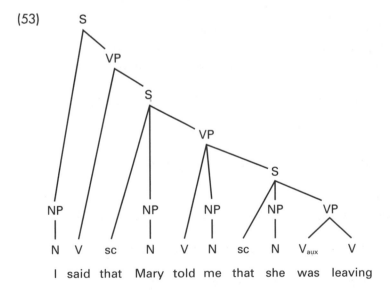

(54) <u>When she arrived</u>, Mary told me <u>that she was leaving</u>.

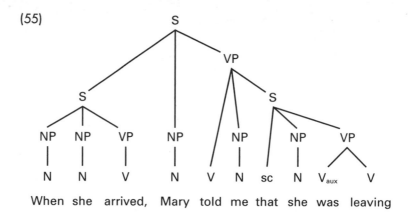

(55)

When she arrived, Mary told me that she was leaving

It is essential to decide which you are dealing with. If one clause is inside the other, then they should be capable of being replaced together, moved together, questioned together, and otherwise sticking together.

(52) I said <u>that Mary told me that she was leaving.</u>

(56) I said this.

(57) What did I say?

Once you have determined that a subordinate sentence is contained inside another subordinate sentence, it should be possible to use the same kinds of test to isolate the most deeply contained sentence.

(52) I said <u>that Mary told me that she was leaving.</u>

(58) I said <u>that Mary told me this</u>.

(59) What did I say <u>that Mary told me</u>?

If the two subordinate sentences are unconnected, it should be possible to manipulate one without affecting the other.

(54) <u>When she arrived</u>, Mary told me <u>that she was leaving</u>.

(60) Mary told me <u>when she arrived</u> <u>that she was leaving</u>.

(61) Mary told me <u>that she was leaving</u> <u>when she arrived</u>.

(62) Mary told me this then.

(63) What did Mary tell you <u>when she arrived</u>?

EXERCISES

7.1 ☞ Practice tree structures for complex sentences

(a) The sentences in this exercise contain two or more main verbs. Underline the main verbs in each case.

(b) Identify the beginning and end of each of the subordinate clauses in each sentence. (In some cases, one subordinate clause is inside another.)

(c) Draw tree structures for these complex sentences.

> (64) He probably wants to leave town before it is too late.
> (65) I promised that the papers would be ready.
> (66) This is the book that I am reading.
> (67) Whenever we go, we should be careful.
> (68) I said that I was intending to leave soon.
> (69) Mary persuaded the woman to read both books.
> (70) It seems that it has rained.
> (71) He saw me walk to the store.
> (72) We can overcome division only by refusing to be divided.

7.2 *The house that Jack built*

Draw a tree structure for the root sentence in (1) at the beginning of this chapter. You will need a large sheet of paper.

7.3 ☞ Accusative subject?

(a) For each of these sentences, use the tests listed in this chapter to identify the beginning and end of the subordinate clause. In particular, is the NP *me* in the root or subordinate clause?

> (73) She persuaded me to eat it.
> (74) She wanted me to eat it.
> (75) She told me to eat it.
> (76) She promised me to eat it.

(b) Speakers of English vary in whether they accept the last of these sentences, (76). Apart from this, what makes it different from the others?

7.4 ☞ *See them running*

(a) A word with the form V+ing, such as *running* or *reading* in the following examples, could in principle be a verb, noun or adjective. Prove its word class in these examples.

(b) Draw tree structures for the sentences.

>   (77) I saw them running.

>   (78) I heard him reading the book to his daughter.

7.5 *To be or not to be*

Draw a diagram of the root and subordinate sentence structure of the sentences in this example. Bear in mind that *or* is a coordinating conjunction which joins two constituents of the same kind and makes the same kind and level of constituent from them.

>   (79) To be, or not to be. That is the question.
>   Whether 'tis nobler in the mind to suffer
>   The slings and arrows of outrageous fortune,
>   Or to take arms against a sea of troubles,
>   And by opposing end them?

7.6 *Though*

Draw tree structures for the following sentences. What do they tell you about the word class of *though*?

>   (80) The dog was happy though wet.

>   (81) The dog was happy though we were not.

7.7 *So*

(a) Examine the following sentences, and for each sentence, decide what the word class of *so* is. It may differ from sentence to sentence.

(b) Draw tree structures for the sentences.

>   (82) He was so in a rage that we had to leave.

>   (83) It was so big a box that we had to knock part of the wall down.

>   (84) He did so.

>   (85) So he did!

>   (86) We did it so as to leave him some food.

(87) We did it so that he would have some food.

(88) So what?

7.8 ☞ Markers of cohesion and their syntactic class

A sequence of root sentences is a discourse. Root sentences can be connected to other root sentences by various phrases, which in discourse analysis are called CONNECTIVES. Each of these phrases has a syntactic word class.

Connectives

(a) For each of the following sentences, say what the class is of each phrase (it could be noun phrase, adverb phrase, adjective phrase or preposition phrase).

(b) Justify your answer by referring to the appropriate tests.

(89) They *nevertheless* decided to leave town.

(90) *In fact* it soon collapsed.

(91) *Therefore* I conclude that they entered by the back.

7.9 The locations of *not*

The sentences in this exercise illustrate different places where *not* can be put. Draw tree structures for the sentences, and try to explain why putting *not* in each place has the effect that it does.

(92) John is not saying that Mary left.

(93) John is saying that Mary did not leave.

(94) John is saying not that Mary left but that Sally left.

(95) John is saying that not Mary but Sally left.

(96) Not John but Peter is saying that Mary left.

7.10 ☞ *Because* and *and*

Apply tests to show that *because* is a subordinating conjunction at the beginning of the subordinate clause, while *and* is a coordinating conjunction which joins two root clauses.

(97) John left because Mary left.

(98) John left and Mary left.

7.11 ☞ *I consider the weather nice*

(a) Use tests to determine whether [*the weather nice*] is a constituent in the following sentence.

(b) If it is a constituent, what kind of constituent is it?

(99) I consider the weather nice.

7.12 Subordinate clauses in other languages

Draw tree structures for the following sentences from the corpus (all of which involve subordinate clauses):

Chinese: J1, J2

Madi: J1, J3

Malay: J1, J2

Tamil: J2, J3

MEANING AND FORM

8

The phrases in a sentence contribute in a systematic way to the meaning of the sentence. While there is a relation between the structural location of a phrase and its contribution to the meaning, it is also possible to change the structure of a sentence in ways which leave some aspects of the meaning unchanged.

THEMATIC ROLES

A sentence represents an eventuality, and the component parts of the sentence can be thought of as representing component parts of the eventuality. We now make this rough sketch from Chapter 5 slightly more precise by looking at the way in which a verb relates to noun phrases and other types of phrase in the sentence.

(1)   Kes ate a nice piece of fish yesterday.

▶   **Draw a tree structure for this sentence.**

The type of eventuality here is eating, as expressed by the verb *eat*. The things involved in the eventuality are *Kes* and *a nice piece of fish*, represented by the two noun phrases. The phrase *yesterday* tells us about the circumstance of the eventuality. This distinction between type, things involved, and circumstances, is a useful three-way division of a sentence's meaning. (To get some practice in dividing the sentence up in this way, do Exercise 8.1.)

The technical term for the types of eventuality is the PREDICATOR. (NB this is not the same as predicate, p. 35, which usually refers to the whole verb phrase, not the verb on its own.) The technical term for the things involved in the eventuality is ARGUMENTS. The predicator-argument(s) structure of this sentence could be represented like this.

Predicator

Arguments

(2) ate   = predicator
     Kes   = argument 1
     a nice piece of fish   = argument 2

Transitive

Because the predicator has two arguments it is called TRANSITIVE. An intransitive predicator has only one argument; an example would be *sleep* as in *She slept*. A ditransitive predicator has three arguments; an example would be *gave* as in *She gave him the book* or *She gave the book to him*.

When the verb *eat* has two arguments, one of them refers to the eater, who could also be called the agent of the action. The other argument refers to the thing eaten, which could more abstractly be called the patient of the action. Terms such as agent or patient describe what is **Thematic role** called the THEMATIC ROLE or theta-role of the arguments relative to the predicator.

(3) ate   = predicator
     Kes   = argument 1 = agent
     a nice piece of fish   = argument 2 = patient

Other thematic roles which arguments can play relative to the predicator include goal (where something goes), instrument (something with which something is done), causer (makes something happen but not intentionally, a kind of inanimate agent), experiencer (undergoes an experience), and so on. These are ways of classifying the kinds of relation which an argument can have relative to a predicator.

STRUCTURAL REARRANGEMENTS WHICH DO NOT SIGNIFICANTLY AFFECT MEANING

It is possible to find two sentences with the same argument structures, but organized into different tree structures. Here are two such sentences; both have the same predicator and the same arguments.

(1) Kes ate a nice piece of fish yesterday.

(4) A nice piece of fish was eaten by Kes yesterday.

▶ **Draw a tree structure for the sentence in (4).**

One way of representing the difference between these sentences is in the relation between grammatical roles (such as subject and object) and thematic roles (such as agent and patient).

	subject	object	by-phrase
(1)	Agent	Patient	
	(Kes)	(a nice piece of fish)	
(4)	Patient		Agent
	(a nice piece of fish)		(Kes)

This is a characteristic difference between sentences which are ACTIVE like (1) and sentences which are PASSIVE like (4); the thematic role played by the object in the active sentence is played instead by the subject in the passive sentence. The active–passive difference permits essentially the same eventuality to be expressed in different kinds of sentence structure. It is possible that the difference involves the relative prominence of the arguments; the active makes the agent more prominent and the passive de-emphasizes the agent and makes the patient more prominent. Some more examples of sentences which have similar meanings but different arrangements of thematic roles are seen in Exercise 8.2 and Exercise 8.3.

Active
Passive

MOVEMENT TO THE FRONT (THE LEFT EDGE) OF THE SENTENCE

The rearrangements of arguments discussed in the previous section do not significantly alter the overall structure of the sentence; thus there is still one NP (the subject) before the verb, whether this carries a thematic role of agent or patient. We now look at the possibility of adding material before the subject of the sentence.

(5)   A nice piece of fish Kes ate yesterday. [as a sentence]

(6)   A nice piece of fish, Kes ate it yesterday.

In these sentences (both of which require the right intonation pattern to make them sound acceptable) the patient argument is put at the beginning of the sentence, before the subject. This is called TOPICALIZATION, and the fronted phrase is called the topic. Notice that the topicalized NP can be recapitulated by a pronoun in the position from which it came (here, object position). Topicalization of this kind is somewhat marginal in some dialects of English; if you don't like these sentences, try the shorter *Fish, Kes likes*. Another dialectal variant of topicalization is shown in Exercise 8.5. In the simplified sentence structures we use here, we will put topicalized phrases at the beginning of the sentence:

Topicalization

(7)

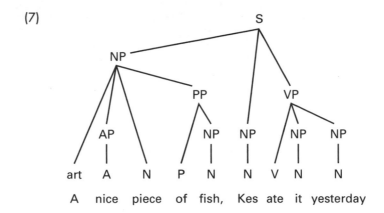

A nice piece of fish, Kes ate it yesterday

WH-QUESTIONS

All the sentences we have seen so far are declarative sentences, which state something. In contrast a sentence which asks a question is interrogative. One way of asking a question is to direct the question to a constituent of a sentence, in the expectation that the answer will relate specifically to this constituent. A constituent is questioned by replacing **Wh-phrase** it with a WH-PHRASE and moving it to the front of the sentence (i.e. topicalizing it). A wh-phrase is a phrase containing a wh-word; they are italicized in (8)–(13). The process is called wh-movement, and in these examples the wh-movement creates wh-questions, also called information questions.

(8)   *What* did you see?

(9)   *Which person* is most likely to have come?

(10)   *Whose book* is this?

(11)   *Who* wants pizza?

(12)   *Which box* did you put the presents in?

(13)   *In which box* did you put the presents?

For the purposes of this book we treat the wh-phrase as at the beginning of the root sentence, and so write a tree structure like this:

(14)

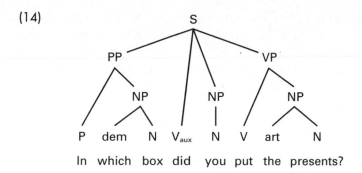

In which box did you put the presents?

Wh-movement is quite strange in some respects. First, note that the movement pulls up other material along with it. For example the movement of the NP *which box* in (13) pulls up the whole PP which contains the NP (a phenomenon called pied piping). This is optional; it doesn't happen in (12). Second, wh-movement can take the phrase out of a subordinate sentence into a higher sentence. In (15) the noun phrase *which book* is the object of the subordinate verb *read* and has nothing to do with the root verb *say* even though it is at the front of the root sentence.

(15) *Which book* did you say the person read?

Many syntactic discoveries have involved these peculiarities of wh-movement. To give a hint of the issues discussed, consider the fact that while it is possible to move a wh-phrase out of a subordinate clause to the beginning of a root clause, this is NOT possible when the subordinate clause is a relative clause inside a noun phrase, as in the following example.

(16) **Which book* did you meet the person who read?

The example is ungrammatical and comes across as incoherent but it is not immediately clear why this should be. Questions such as *why is this sentence ungrammatical?* are the kinds of question which arise once we stop just accepting language as a given, and start asking why it is as it is.

YES-NO QUESTIONS

Wh-questions are one kind of question in English. The other kind of question is a YES-NO QUESTION, so called because it can be answered by *yes* or by *no* rather than by giving information. A yes-no question can be created by taking an ordinary (declarative) sentence and giving it a particular intonation pattern, most characteristically with a rising

Yes-no question

intonation at the end. Thus for example the statement *You ate* could be the question *You ate?* An alternative way of making a yes-no question is to move the tensed verb or auxiliary or modal to the left of (before) the subject. Note that in the tree diagram we have still included a verb phrase in the sentence even though the verb has been moved out of it and to the front of the sentence.

(17) Is Kes sleepy?

(18) Did Kes sleep?

(19)

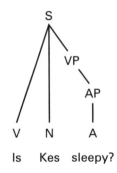

KINDS OF MEANING

An implication of what we have seen in this unit is that there are distinct aspects of a sentence which contribute to its meaning; that is, meaning is not a single unified thing but is multi-dimensional. A fundamental aspect of the meaning of a sentence is its predicator-argument structure: the relation between the predicator and the arguments which together represent an eventuality. Part of this is the identification of the thematic roles played by the arguments relative to the predicator. Thus predicator-argument structure and the thematic role system contribute one strand to the overall meaning of a sentence. But it is also the case that rearrangements such as passive and topicalization also contribute to the meaning of the sentence, perhaps by changing the prominence of information contained in the sentence. And the distinction between a declarative and an interrogative sentence (a statement v. a question) is also a matter of meaning. These different kinds of meaning are interrelated but are distinct from one another.

EXERCISES

8.1 Practice – the components of the eventuality

(a) For each of the sentences below, underline the word expressing the type of eventuality. (For example, in (20) underline *read*.)

(b) Circle the phrases which identify the things involved in the eventuality, bearing in mind the tree structure of the sentence. (For example, in (20) circle *the boy* and *the book*.)

(c) Put a box around the words or phrases which identify the circumstances of the eventuality. (For example, in (20) put a box around *with a heavy heart*.)

(d) Are there any words or phrases in these sentences which you think do not fall into one of these three categories?

> (20) The boy read the book with a heavy heart.
> (21) The girl gave the book to her friends.
> (22) The girl gave Peter the book.
> (23) The girl had never given Peter the book.
> (24) The girl gave the book to Mary and June.
> (25) The girl casually read the book in the afternoon.
> (26) The girl inspected the book with a magnifying glass.

8.2 ☞ Dative shift

Some verbs such as *teach* can permit the same combination of thematic roles to be expressed either by a subject plus an object NP plus a PP, or (in a structure called dative shift) by a subject plus an object NP plus a second object NP.

> (27) We taught Italian to the students.
> (28) We taught the students Italian.

(a) The following verbs can all be followed by NP + PP. Which can also be followed by NP + NP?

teach, donate, sell, buy, tell, throw, demonstrate, gift (as a verb), transfer, send, convey

(b) Is it possible to formulate a generalization about which verbs do not take NP + NP?

8.3 Active, passive and middle

In the following examples, sentence (i) is active, and sentence (ii) is passive. Sentence (iii) shows a third possibility; here the object of the equivalent active sentence is in the subject position (like passive) but there is no auxiliary verb or special passive morphology. Examples like **Middle** (iii) are called MIDDLE.

(29) (i)   The cook melted the ice.

(ii)   The ice was melted (by the cook).

(iii) The ice melted.

(30) (i)   The torpedo sank the boat.

(ii)   The boat was sunk.

(iii) The boat sank.

(31) (i)   Maxine accepted the parcel.

(ii)   The parcel was accepted.

(iii) *The parcel accepted.

(32) (i)   The birds resembled fish.

(ii)   *Fish were resembled.

(iii) *Fish resembled.

(a) Why are some of the above sentences ungrammatical in the middle form (iii)? Test your hypothesis by making up some more examples.

(b) Explain why *The lion killed* cannot mean that the lion ended up dead. (Compare *The boat sank* ((iii) in example (30)) where the boat ends up sunk.)

8.4 ☞ *Get* passives

Instead of (33) it is possible to say (34), with *get* instead of *be*. What is the word class of *get*? Justify your answer.

(33) This book is read a lot (by John).

(34) This book gets read a lot (by John).

8.5 ☞ *See* topicalization

In the dialect of English spoken for example in Glasgow (Scotland), the following topicalization strategy is found. Draw a tree structure for this sentence. You will need to decide what word class *see* is in this sentence.

(35) See the cappuccino, does it have sugar in it?

8.6 ☞ Right-shift

It is usually argued that the italicized phrases in the following examples have been right-shifted – moved to the end (the right edge) of the sentence. Find arguments in favour of this.

(36) I sent to you yesterday *a very large parcel.*

(37) The girl met me *who you called last night.*

(38) It was clear to me *that this was a good idea.*

8.7 ☞ Which main verbs can move in yes-no questions?

An auxiliary or modal verb can always be moved to the left of (before) the subject in a yes-no question. But most main verbs cannot. Find as many examples as you can where main verbs are moved to the left of the subject in a yes-no question. (You can think of dialectal or historical examples if you know any, and examples from literature.)

8.8 ☞ The wh-word in the relative clause

Like an information question, a relative clause can begin with a phrase containing a *wh*-word, which might be argued to have moved. The following noun phrases all contain a relative clause, which has been underlined to help you:

(39) the pictures <u>I offered to her</u>

(40) the pictures <u>that I offered to her</u>

(41) the pictures <u>which I offered to her</u>

(42) the girl <u>who you met</u>

(43) the person <u>whose book I bought</u>

(44) the person <u>for whose sake we did it</u>

(45) the place <u>where we were meeting</u>

(46) the day <u>when you arrived</u>

(a) Circle the word or phrase which comes before the subject inside each relative clause. For example, circle *that* in (40).

(b) How do the subordinate clauses in (41)–(46) differ from root wh-questions such as *who did you meet?* etc.

(c) What class of word is *that* in (40)? Justify your answer, and draw a tree structure for the sentence.

8.9 ☞ *How* questions

In each of the following sentences, *how* or a phrase beginning with *how* functions to subordinate a clause. The subordinate clauses are underlined to help you.

(47) I told her <u>how slowly it took</u>.
(48) I told her <u>how nice they were</u>.
(49) I told her <u>how he looked</u>.

(a) Draw tree structures for (47)–(49). This involves deciding whether *how* is part of a larger phrase at the front of the subordinate clause, or whether it is on its own at the front of the subordinate clause.

(b) What is the word class of *how* in each sentence? It may be different in different sentences.

(c) Is there any justification for saying that the phrase containing *how* has been moved to the beginning of the subordinate clause?

8.10 Information questions in other languages

In different languages, information questions are dealt with differently. For example, the question phrase (*wh*-phrase) may not move, or might move to a position other than the front of the sentence. Examine the languages in the corpus and for each language determine how information questions are formed. You should look particularly at:

Chinese: B1–3

Madi: B1–7

Malay: B1–5

Tamil: B1–10

8.11 Passive in other languages

Not all languages form passive in the same way that English does. Examine the languages in the corpus and for each language.

(a) Determine whether there is a difference in sentence structure (or morphology) between the equivalent of English active/passive sentences.

(b) If there is a difference, describe it.

You should look particularly at:

Chinese: L1, L2

Madi: L1–4

Malay: A2, A3, L1–3

Tamil: A4, L1

8.12 Word order in Tamil

Tamil has fairly free phrase order. Examine the Tamil sentences in the corpus and describe:

(a)   Where the verb typically goes.

(b)   Where the subject and object noun phrases go.

(c)   How the placement of phrases relates to what is being emphasized.

(d)   Why Tamil is able to have freer word order than English.

FURTHER READING

O'Grady, W.D, Katamba, F. and Dobrovolsky, M., *Contemporary Linguistics* (London: Pearson Education, 2001).
Standard introductory textbook for linguistics in general.

Chomsky, N., *Syntactic Structures* (Berlin: Mouton, 1957).
The classic work which introduced 'generative linguistics'. Most of the components of the theory have now been changed, but the fundamental insights remain startling.

Chomsky, N., *On Nature and Language* (Cambridge: Cambridge University Press, 2002).
A collection of short articles and an interview which brings *Syntactic Structures* up to date.

Jackendoff, R., *X-bar syntax: A Study of Phrase Structure* (Cambridge, MA: MIT Press, 1977).
The most influential work on phrase structure ever written, taking the simple account in the present book to a new level of complexity.

Crystal, D., *The Cambridge Encyclopedia of Language* (2nd edition) (Cambridge: Cambridge University Press, 2003).
An illustrated survey of language and linguistics for the general reader.

McArthur, T., *Oxford Guide to World English* (Oxford: Oxford University Press, 2002).
A good value compendium of information about dialects, including 'grammar' (sentence structure).

Huddleston, R. and Pullum, G., *The Cambridge Grammar of the English Language* (Cambridge: Cambridge University Press, 2002).
The grammar which is probably now the standard theoretically informed description of English.

PROJECTS

You should be able to do these projects after completing the book. They involve you in analysing actual sentences. You will find that some are more complicated than the ones analysed in this book, and you will find some problems which we have not addressed (such as words whose word classes you are not sure about); however, you should by now have the basic problem-solving skills to be able to confront and deal with these problems.

1 Different kinds of text typically use different kinds of language, which include different vocabularies and different sentence structures; these differences are called differences in register. You can use your knowledge of sentence structure to explore some of these differences. Here is one way of doing it: pick a poem written in the nineteenth century, a newspaper article written today, and an academic book (e.g. a textbook). Write out the first sentence (not the title) from each text, and draw a tree structure for it. Now do the same with another three texts of the same kind. Do you see any patterns of difference emerging?

2 Choose an English sentence discussed in this book, and get it translated into another language. Can the sentence be translated word-for-word (in the same order)? There are likely to be some differences; try to work out what those differences tell you about more general differences between English and the other language. This exercise can be repeated many times; it will give you one way of beginning to understand the structure of the second language.

3 Look at a guide to English usage or a school grammar, and examine in particular the sentences which you are advised not to use. Try to explain why the guide advises you not to use a particular type of sentence. Draw a tree structure for an example of the forbidden sentence type, and

compare it with a tree structure of an acceptable version of the sentence. Is it possible to show that one sentence is better than the other on the basis of the structural difference between them? For example, can you show that one structure is more effective at communicating its meaning than the other? This exercise can be repeated many times. Note that some people think that there are no value differences of this kind between sentences; this exercise should give you a basis for coming to a decision by yourself.

4 Different dialects of English can differ in a number of ways, most obviously in accent – the pronunciation of the language – and in vocabulary. There may also be some differences in sentence structure between two dialects of English. Try to find equivalent sentences from two dialects which are structurally different (e.g. the words or phrases are in a different order). Draw a tree structure for each sentence, and describe the difference in syntactic terms (e.g. discuss word class, generalizations about order, processes such as movement which might be involved, and so on). You might find the *Oxford Guide to World English* (see further reading) useful to give you some clues as to what to look for in your own dialect.

SENTENCES FROM OTHER LANGUAGES

HOW TO USE THE FOUR CORPORA WHICH FOLLOW

A corpus is a representative collection of things, and the four corpuses (or 'corpora') which follow present collections of relatively simple sentences from four different kinds of language. For each language, sentences are given with rough English translations of what the sentence as a whole means. In order to work with the sentences, you need to decide what the individual words mean. As you work through each corpus, write the English word under the equivalent foreign language word, if possible. Often a word will correspond exactly with an English word, but some English words like *the* may not correspond to a word in the other language; similarly, other languages may have words which have no corresponding words in English.

The strategy you should use for working out the meaning and function of individual words is to compare sentences which differ minimally from each other. For example, if you were working on Madi you could take the sentences A2 and A3:

A2   otse re odi au re ra   The dog killed the chicken.

A3   otse re onya au re ra   The dog ate the chicken.

The difference in the Madi sentences is that A2 uses *odi* and A3 uses *onya*; the corresponding difference in the English translations is that A2 uses *killed* and A3 uses *ate*. So *odi* probably means 'killed' and *onya* probably means 'ate'. It would be a reasonable guess, unless you had reason to think otherwise, that *odi* and *onya* are verbs, because *killed* and *ate* are verbs too. Use this approach as a general strategy for getting to grips with the languages.

Notice that from these examples you do *not* have evidence that *otse re* means 'the dog', even though *otse re* is at the beginning of the sentence and *the dog* is at the beginning of its sentence. You can however get evidence by comparing A1 with A3:

A1   ebi re onya au re ra   The fish ate the chicken.

A3   otse re onya au re ra   The dog ate the chicken.

Since the difference here is in the word *ebi* v. *otse* which corresponds to a difference in the translation of *fish* v. *dog* you have good evidence that *ebi* means 'fish' and *otse* means 'dog'.

A note on the examples

Examples from languages other than English are written using the so-called 'roman' alphabet which is used for English. I have not used other standard writing systems (the Arabic examples are not written in arabic script, for example), and I have not used anything approaching a phonetic script (tones are ignored, too). This is for convenience of sentence structure analysis, but it means that you will only get a rough sense from looking at the examples of how the words are pronounced. This is true for the examples throughout the book. I take responsibility for any errors in the examples.

A few comments on the corpus sentences

The comments made above about transcription of words hold true also for these sentences. Only Malay has a standardized roman orthography for its words; for the other languages, the native speakers who gave me the sentences have suggested how to write the words down. Inevitably certain things are lost: Tamil for example has many spoken consonants not found in English and so is not well represented by roman letters, while Chinese and Madi are both languages in which the tone of the words is a central part of their meaning.

Because these sentences have been chosen to provide fairly simple support for the material discussed in the units (which are oriented towards English), I have avoided using complex examples, or examples which raise too many problems. The simplicity of the examples should not give the impression that the languages are in any way simple.

Adding your own language

You may know another language, in which case it would be simple to write your own list of about 30 to 50 sentences, rough equivalents to the sentences given here. You could then use these sentences in the various corpus-based exercises in this book and so adapt the end-of-unit exercises to explore this new language.

CHINESE (CANTONESE)

These examples were provided by Toh Guat Choon and Kon Yoon How. There are many different dialects within Chinese, of which the best known is probably Mandarin. The examples here are from Cantonese. As an example of differences between different dialects of Chinese, the first sentence might be:

yu sik choa kó chaet kai	A fish ate that chicken.	(Cantonese dialect)
ng sik hoi ai chaek kai	A fish ate that chicken.	(Hakka dialect)
hu chiak liau hi chiak kay	A fish ate that chicken.	(Hokkien dialect)

(The words in each dialect are in the same order; the differences here are in the word chosen for each meaning.)

Note:

(a)   Chinese has classifiers; *chaet* in sentence A5 is an example of one (annotated as cl.).

(b)   Chinese is a language where words are differentiated by tone (whether the voice rises, falls, etc., while saying the vowel). This is indicated for just two words below: kó and kò, to indicate that they are different words.

A   Simple transitive sentence

(1)   kao chui kai — A dog chases a chicken.

(2)   kao sik kai — A dog eats a chicken.

(3)   yu sik kai — A fish eats a chicken.
      fish eat chicken

(4)   yu sik choa kai — A fish ate a chicken.

(5)   yu sik choa kó chaet kai — A fish ate that chicken.
      fish eat past that cl.   chicken

B   Questions

(1)   sai louchai sik choa kó teeu tai yu — Small children ate that large fish.

(2)   pinko sik choa kó teeu tai yu — Who ate that large fish?

(3)   sai louchai sik choa matye — What did children eat?

(4)   sai louchai yau sik choa kó teeu tai yu mo — Did children eat that large fish?

(5)   sai louchai wooi sik kó teeu tai yu mo — Will children eat that large fish?

C   Full NP compared with pronoun

(1)   kó kò luiyan mai choa kó tong gau chei   That woman bought that old car.

(2)   hei mai choa chei   She/he bought a car.

D   Inside an NP (and attributive/predicative phrases)

(1)   ngo sik choa tai teeu yu   I ate a big fish.
(2)   ngo sik choa yat teeu tai yu   I ate one big fish.
(3)   ngo sik choa leong teeu tai yu   I ate two big fish.
(4)   ngo sik choa mui teeu yu   I ate every fish.
(5)   heitei sik choa kó kò yan kei yu   They ate that person's fish.
(6)   ngo gindo kó kò yan   I saw that person.
(7)   ngo gindo li kò yan   I saw this person.
(8)   kó kò yan ho seongsam   That person is very sad.
(9)   yat kò ho seongsam yan sik chao mui teeu yu   One very sad person ate every fish.

F   PP

(1)   ngo fong kó poon shu hai toi sheongpin   I put that book on the desk. ('put' = present tense here.)

(2)   kó poon shu hai toi sheongpin   That book is on the desk.
(3)   ngo fong kó poon shu hai toi yappin   I put that book in the desk.
(4)   kó poon shu hai toi yappin   That book is in the desk.
(5)   hei heong okkei yappin   She is in the house.
(6)   hei heong okkei chokung   She works in the house.

G   Auxiliaries, tense and modals

(1)   hei sik yu   He eats a fish.
(2)   hei sik choa yu   He ate a fish.
(3)   hei yau sik yu   He *did* eat a fish (emphasized).

(4)   hei hohnang sik choa yu   He might eat a fish.
(5)   hei wooi sik yu   He will eat a fish.

H   *Not*

(1)   kao m sik kai   A dog does not eat a chicken.

(2)   hei m hohnang sik yu   He cannot eat a fish (i.e. there is no possibility of it).

J   Subordinate sentence

(1)   hei wa kó chaet kai ho tai

He said that chicken was very big.

(2)   hei seongsam yanwai kao sei chao   He was sad because a dog died.

K   Coordination

(1)   kao sik choa yu tung kai

The dog ate the fish and the chicken.

L   Passive

(1)   kao chui choa kai   A dog chased a chicken.
(2)   kai pei kao chui choa   A chicken was chased by a dog.

MADI

Madi is a language of the Central Sudanic group. It is spoken in Southern Sudan and Northern Uganda. For a full account of this language, see Blackings, M. and Fabb, N., *A Grammar of Ma'di*, 2003, Berlin: Mouton de Gruyter. The language is a tone language, which means that important information is carried in the tones on the words; however, these are not indicated in these examples.

Note:

    (a)   *ra* at the end of a sentence means 'definitely' (i.e. what is said is definitely true).

    (b)   The pronoun subject merges with a verb, and can lead to a change in the verb; e.g. *ma* ('I') combines with *odze* ('buy') to give *madze* ('I buy').

A   Simple transitive sentence

(1)   ebi re onya au re ra   The fish ate the chicken.
(2)   otse re odi au re ra   The dog killed the chicken.
(3)   otse re onya au re ra   The dog ate the chicken.
(4)   borondzi re onya ki ebi amgbugodru re ra adzini

The children ate the large fish yesterday.

(5)   bara re onya ebi amgbugodru re ra adzini

The child ate the large fish yesterday.

(6)   borondzi re onya ki ebi amgbugodru re ra adzini

The children ate the large fish yesterday.

(7)   borondzi re onya ki ebi amgbugodru re adzini ra

The children ate the large fish yesterday.

(8)	adzini borondzi re onya ki ebi amgbugodru re ra	The children ate the large fish yesterday.
(9)	madze arabia adzini re ra	I bought the car which we spoke about yesterday.

B   Questions

(1)	borondzi re onya ki ebi amgbugodru re ra adzini	The children ate the large fish yesterday.
(2)	adi onya ebi amgbugodru re adzini ni	Who ate the large fish yesterday?
(3)	adu ba onya ki ebi amgbugodru re adzini ni	Which person ate the large fish yesterday?
(4)	borondzi re onya ki adu adzini	What did the children eat yesterday?
(5)	borondzi re onya ki ebi amgbugodru re adu nggani	When did the children eat the large fish?
(6)	ebi amgbugodru re, borondzi re onya adu nggani	The large fish, when did the children eat it?
(7)	borondzi re onya ki ebi amgbugodru re inggo	Where did the children eat the large fish?

C   Full NP compared with pronoun

(1)	ago re odze arabia re ra	The man bought the car.
(2)	madze arabia re ra	I bought the car.
(3)	mande ani adzini	I saw him/her yesterday.
(4)	mande bara re adzini	I saw the child yesterday.

D   Inside an NP (and attributive/predicative phrases)

(1)	ebi na amgbugodru	A fish is large.
(2)	ebi re amgbugodru ambaba	The fish is very large.
(3)	ebi di amgbugodru	This fish is large.
(4)	manya ago re a au ra	I ate the man's chicken.

E   More complex NPs

(1)	madze kwe ni eno udi re ra	I bought a new picture of the tree.
(2)	madze eno udi, obga laka kwe eri	I bought a new picture, drawn on it were two trees.
(3)	magba kwe ni eno	I drew a picture of the tree.

F PP

(1) magba brasi si — I painted with a brush.
(2) maba buku re teremeza re ni dri — I put the book on the table.

H *Not*

(1) odi au re ku ru — The chicken was not killed.
(2) otse re odi au re ni ku — It was specifically not the *dog* which killed the chicken.

J Subordinate sentence

(1) ojo ani kemu obu — He/She said he/she comes tomorrow.
(2) ojo nyimu obu — He/She said you go tomorrow.
(3) mani ra ebi re ibwe — I know (definitely) the fish is cold.
(4) majo ebi re ibwe — I said the fish is cold.

K Coordination

(1) ama dzi arabia re pi gari re tro su ga — We took the car and bicycle to the market. (Note: *pi* means 'and', *tro* means 'with'.)
(2) ago re pi izi re tro ovu ki su ga — The man and the woman walked to the market (note the plural).

L Passive

(1) odi au re ra — The chicken was killed.
(2) au re odi ra — The chicken was killed.
(3) au re onya ra — The chicken was eaten.
(4) onya au re ra — The chicken was eaten.

M Specifically

(1) otse re onya au re ni — Specifically the dog ate the chicken.

N Location

(1) manya linya ra — I have eaten food.
(2) menya linya ra — I ate food (i.e. before coming).

MALAY

The examples in this section are from standard spoken Malay (Bahasa Melayu). They were provided by Wan Faiezah Megat Noordin and Yasmin Osman.

A Simple transitive sentence

(1) ikan ini telah makan ayam itu   This fish ate the chicken.
(2) anjing ini telah membunuh ayam itu This dog killed the chicken.
(3) anjing ini telah makan ayam itu   This dog ate the chicken.

B Questions

(1) budak-budak kecil itu telah makan ikan besar itu semalam — The young children ate the large fish yesterday.
(2) semalam budak-budak kecil itu telah makan ikan besar itu — The young children ate the large fish yesterday?
(3) siapa telah makan ikan besar itu — Who ate the large fish?
(4) apa yang telah dimakan oleh budak-budak kecil itu — What was eaten by the young children?
(5) bila budak-budak itu makan ikan itu — When did the children eat the fish?
(6) adakah budak-budak kecil itu makan ikan besar itu semalam? — Did the young children eat the large fish yesterday?

C Full NP compared with pronoun

(1) lelaki itu telah beli kereta itu   The man bought the car.
(2) dia telah beli kereta itu   He bought the car.
(3) saya nampak dia   I saw him/her.

D Inside an NP (and attributive/predicative phrases)

(1) lelaki itu gembira   The man is happy.
(2) lelaki itu sedih   The man is sad.
(3) lelaki yang gembira itu makan ikan itu — The happy man ate the fish.
(4) lelaki itu makan seekor ikan yang besar — The man ate a large fish.
(5) seorang lelaki sedang makan ikan itu — A/One man is eating the fish.
(6) seorang lelaki telah makan ikan itu A man ate the fish.
(7) dua orang lelaki telah makan seekor ayam — Two men ate a chicken.

(8)	dua ekor ayam telah makan semua ikan itu	Two chickens ate all the fish.
(9)	tiga ekor ayam telah makan separuh ikan itu	Three chickens ate half of the fish.
(10)	kami nampak kereta lelaki ini	We saw this man's car.

F PP (and the word *ada*)

(1)	saya ada buku itu	I have the book.
(2)	lelaki itu ada disini	The man is here.
(3)	lelaki itu ada disana	The man is over there.
(4)	buku ini ada di atas meja	This book is on the desk.
(5)	saya letak buku itu di atas meja	I put the book on the desk.
(6)	saya letak buku itu didalam meja	I put the book inside the desk.

G Auxiliaries, tense and modals

(1)	lelaki itu gembira	That/The man is happy.
(2)	dulu lelaki itu gembira	That/The man used to be happy.
(3)	lelaki itu dulu, gembira	That/The man used to be happy.
(4)	* akan lelaki itu gembira	That/The man will be happy. (Note: an ungrammatical sentence.)
(5)	lelaki itu akan gembira	That/The man will be happy.
(6)	lelaki itu pasti gembira	That/The man is sure to be happy.

H Not

(1)	anjing ini tidak makan ayam itu	This dog did not eat the chicken.
(2)	anjing ini tidak akan makan ayam itu	This dog will not eat the chicken.
(3)	anjing ini tidak makan ayam	This dog does not eat chicken.

J Subordinate sentence

| (1) | dia kata dia nampak anjing itu semalam | He said he saw the dog yesterday. |
| (2) | dia sedih sebab dia nampak anjing itu semalam | He was sad because he saw the dog yesterday. |

K Coordination

| (1) | saya telah makan tiga ekor ikan dan dua ekor ayam | I ate three fish and two chickens. |
| (2) | mereka telah makan ikan atau ayam | They ate the fish or the chickens. |

L   Passive

(1)	ayam itu telah dibunuh	The chicken was killed.
(2)	ayam itu telah dibunuh oleh anjing itu	The chicken was killed by the dog.
(3)	ayam itu telah dimakan	The chicken was eaten.

TAMIL

These examples are from spoken Tamil, provided by a speaker of Tamil from Malaysia (Malaysian Indian), Rajathilagam a/l Krishnan.

Note: the use of hyphens inside a word (e.g. *koli-ai*) indicates the presence of a suffix which is particularly relevant to understanding the sentence.

A   Simple transitive sentence

(1)	meen koli-ai saapit-ethe	*The fish* ate the chicken (i.e. emphasis on fish).
(2)	koli-ai meen saapit-ethe	The fish ate *the chicken*.
(3)	koli meen-ai saapit-ethe	The chicken ate the fish.
(4)	nai koli-ai kondr-ethe	The dog killed the chicken.
(5)	naigel koli-ai kondr-ener	The dogs killed the chicken.
(6)	pillai koli-ai kondr-ethe	The child killed the chicken.
(7)	pillaigel koli-ai kondr-ener	The children killed the chicken.
(8)	nai koli-ai saapit-ethe	The dog ate the chicken.

B   Questions

(1)	neetre antha pillaigel antha periya meen-ai saapit-ener	Yesterday those children ate that big fish.
(2)	yaar neetre antha periya meen-ai saapit-ethe	Who ate that big fish yesterday? ('who' = 'which *singular* person')
(3)	neetre yaar antha periya meen-ai saapit-ener	Who ate that big fish yesterday? (here 'who' = 'which *plural* people')
(4)	neetre antha periya meen-ai yaar saapit-ethe	Who ate that big fish yesterday? ('who' = 'which *singular* person')
(5)	neetre antha pillaigel yethai saapit-ener	What did the children eat yesterday?
(6)	neetre yethai antha pillaigel saapit-ener	What did the children eat yesterday?
(7)	yethai neetre antha pillaigel saapit-ener	What did the children eat yesterday?

(8) yeppoluthu antha pillaigel antha periya meen-ai saapit-ener — When did *the children* eat the large fish?

(9) antha pillaigel yeppoluthu antha periya meen-ai saapit-ener — *When* did the children eat the large fish?

(10) antha pillaigel antha periya meen-ai yeppoluthu saapit-ener — When did the children eat *the large fish*?

(11) neetre antha pillaigel antha periya meen-ai saapit-ener-aa — Did the children eat the large fish yesterday?

C Full NP compared with pronoun

(1) avaar antha gaadi-ai vaangi-naar — The man bought that car.

(2) naan antha gaadi-ai vaangi-nain — I bought that car.

(3) aval antha gaadi-ai vaangi-nal — She bought that car.

(4) neetre aval aathai vaangi-nal — She bought it (i.e. the car) yesterday.

D Inside an NP (and attributive/predicative phrases)

(1) naan oru siriye veed-ai vaangi-nain — I bought a small house.

(2) naan oru siriye veed-ai vaangi-nain — I bought one small house.

(3) naan irandu siriye veedu-galai vaangi-nain — I bought two small houses.

(4) naan antha miga siriye veed-ai vaangi-nain — I bought that very small house.

(5) naan intha siriye veed-ai vaangi-nain — I bought this small house.

(6) naan mano-vin veed-ai vaangi-nain — I bought Mano's house.

(7) naan mano-vin siriye veed-ai vaangi-nain — I bought Mano's small house.

(8) inthe veedu siriyethu — This house is small.

(9) anthe veedu miga siriyethu — That house is very small.

(10) anthe veedu konjum siriyethu — That house is quite small.

E More complex NPs

(1) naan oru maraan-galin padathai vaangi-nain — I bought a picture of the tree.

(2) naan oru puthiya maraan-galin padathai vaangi-nain — I bought a picture of the new trees.

F PP

(1) naan buthagathai maijain mel vaithain — I put the book on the desk.

(2)	naan buthagathai maijain ullai vaithain	I put the book in the desk.

G   Auxiliaries, tense and modals

(1)	meen koli-ai saapide kindrethe	The fish is eating the chicken.
(2)	meen koli-ai saapide modiyum	The fish can eat chicken.

H   *Not*

(1)	meen koli-ai saapide villai	The fish did not eat the chicken.

J   Subordinate sentence

(1)	avar sonnar naan antha koli-ye paarthathaage	He said I saw the chicken.
(2)	avar naan antha koli-ye paarthathaage sonnar	He said I saw the chicken.
(3)	naan antha koli-ye paartha-thaal avar-ku vartham	Because I saw the chicken he was sorry.
(4)	naan antha koli-ye paarthain	I saw the chicken.
(5)	nai koli-ye kondra-thaal antha pillai-ku vartham	Because the dog killed the chicken, the child was sorry.

K   Coordination

(1)	avar meen-ai-yum koli-ai-yum saapit-ar	He ate the fish and the chicken.
(2)	meen-yum koli-yum puchigel-ai saapit-ener	The fish and the chicken ate the insects.

L   Passive

(1)	koli-ye nai kondr-ethe	The chicken was killed by the dog.

SUGGESTED ANSWERS TO SELECTED EXERCISES

CHAPTER 1 PHRASES

1.1 Alternatives are as follows. (19) *The parcel for Toby* (e.g. addressed to him) OR *the parcel* is being untied *for Toby*. (20) *The ping-pong ball under the sofa* is what is being pushed OR *the ping-pong ball* is being pushed *under the sofa*. (21) *The visitor from Glasgow* (= visiting from Glasgow) OR *the visitor* is being driven *from Glasgow*.

1.2 *The book* and *tomorrow* are two different phrases.

1.4 (a) Eaje + ke noin-i + chorok saek kong-el + peter-ei aidel-ege + ju-eatsepnida. (b) Free phrase order because the words clearly stick together into clumps.

1.5 (29) (a) (structurally grammatical, but forbidden as a written sentence because it begins with *and*)

(30) (a) (grammatical even though it is untrue)

(31) (b) (grammatical e.g. in Scottish dialects)

(32) (a) (grammatical in all dialects even though forbidden because it ends with a preposition)

(33) (b) (grammatical in some dialects)

(34) (c) (ungrammatical because the reflexive *himself* is too far from the phrase it refers to)

(35) (c) (ungrammatical)

(36) (b) (grammatical e.g. in Pakistani dialects)

(37) (a) (grammatical despite the swearword which by itself has nothing to do with grammaticality, though it does affect acceptability)

(38) (c) (ungrammatical because of the impossible order of *is* and *might*).

CHAPTER 2 WORD CLASS AND PHRASE CLASS: THE NOUN PHRASE

2.1 You should find it hard to add a new pronoun, preposition, article or demonstrative; these are the clearest examples of closed classes.

2.4 (a) The noun has stress on the first syllable, and the verb has stress on the second syllable; there are several other words with the same pattern. (b) The voiced sound comes at the beginning of closed class words (article, demonstrative, numeral) and the voiceless at the beginning of open class words.

2.5 Numerals can be pluralized as in *thousands* which suggests that they are nouns; a numeral can be preceded by an article and an adjective, again suggesting that it is a noun, as in *a whole hundred*.

CHAPTER 3 MORE CLASSES OF PHRASE: ADJECTIVE PHRASE, ADVERB PHRASE AND PREPOSITION PHRASE

3.1 Tree structures shown below.

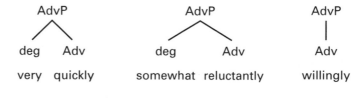

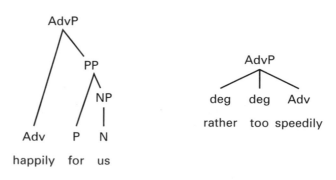

3.2 You should find that the adverb phrase will not go inside the NP or PP (except when it is further embedded inside the AP with *red* as in *The violently red car swerved out of the way*).

3.3 (a) both (b) both (c) iii.

3.4 Tree structures shown below.

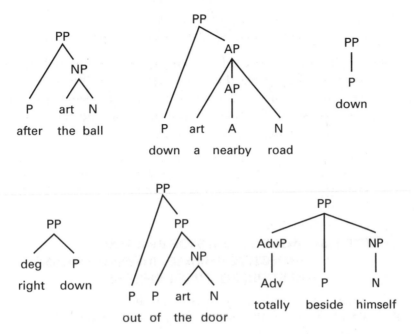

3.5 Some do not obviously express location in time or space: *of* and *as* and perhaps *with* and *without*.

3.6 We know that for most kinds of word, the phrase can contain just the head word. Thus we might expect a PP to contain just a preposition, and this would be exemplified by these. This answer maximizes generalizations across word classes; it means the so-called particles are in effect intransitive prepositions, prepositions without objects.

3.9 *Enough* comes after the adjective which it modifies; degree modifiers usually come before.

CHAPTER 4   THE VERB, THE VERB PHRASE AND THE AUXILIARIES

4.3 This structure explains why *reading the letter to John* can be treated as a consituent on its own (e.g. in movement, deletion).

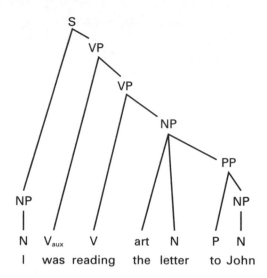

4.4 *Laughing* would have to go into a phrase of some kind within the NP; major class words do not appear bare inside a phrase of another kind.

4.5 (38) *necessary* modal adjective
(39) *might* modal verb; *possibly* modal adverb
(40) *possibility* modal noun. (Note that the word *modality* is not itself a modal word!)

4.7 *Never* is an adverb, as can be seen by the fact that it can be freely moved around; it is similar in distribution and kind of meaning to *sometimes* and *always*.

CHAPTER 5 THE SIMPLE SENTENCE AND ITS TREE STRUCTURE

5.1 (a) one (b) NP (c) three (d) three (e) fourteen (f) one

5.2

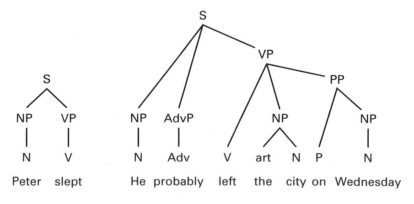

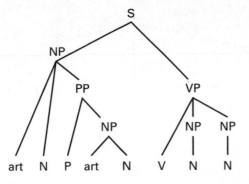

The men on the train gave us tickets

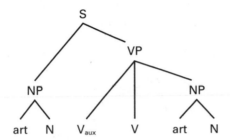

The dogs were attacking the snake

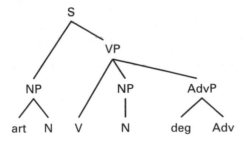

The cats eat breakfast really slowly

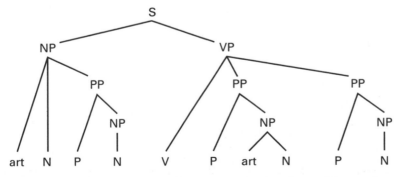

The men with beards walked across the garden without shoes

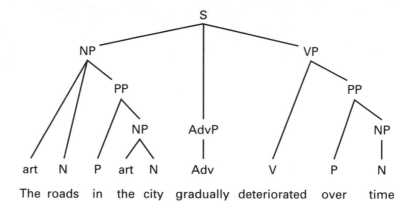

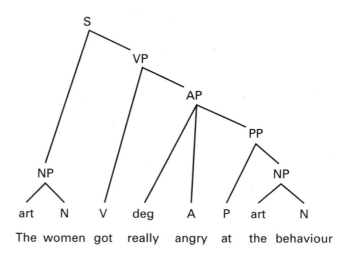

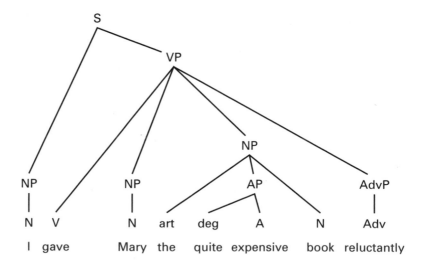

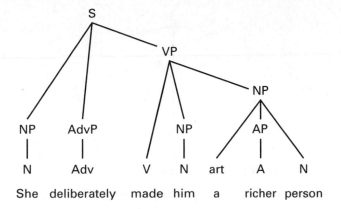

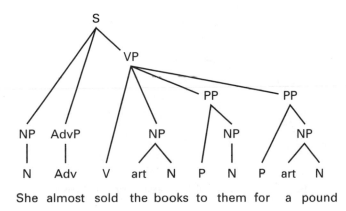

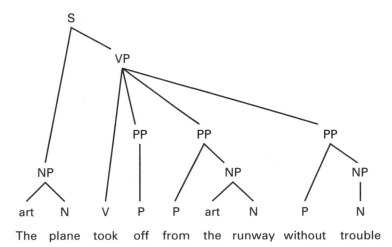

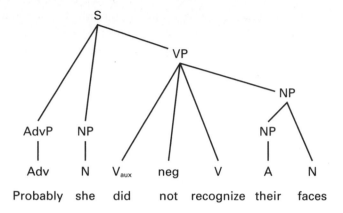

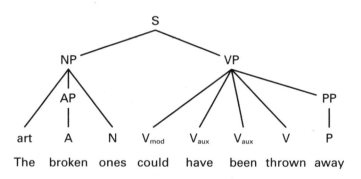

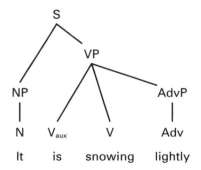

5.5   You should find two distinct kinds of pattern. In some compounds such as noun+noun or adjective+noun compounds, the first word seems to be a modifier of the second word (though these compounds vary in how transparent this relation is). In other compounds – called 'verbal compounds' or 'synthetic compounds' – the first word is treated as the object of the second word, as in 'meat-eater', as though the compound is an inverted verb phrase.

CHAPTER 6   NOUN PHRASES

6.1   (c) *Mary* has a possessive relation to *cat*. *The terrified crow* is the producer rather than the owner of the screech; the same might be said of *my* and *opinion*. *The building* is the thing which is captured.

6.2   The suffix comes at the end of the noun phrase, and need not attach to a noun.

6.4   In two of these dialects there is a demonstrative *them* or *they* which is homophonous with a word otherwise used as a pronoun. In the third, a word which elsewhere is a singular demonstrative *that* is here used with a plural noun.

6.6   An NP cannot just contain an article but it can contain just an article and an adjective as in *the poorest*. All the other types of NP can contain just the beginning word or phrase.

6.8   (b) The sequences seen here are:

(32)   genitive + num + N

(33)   Q + num + N

(34)   genitive + Q + N

(35)   art + num + N

(36)   art + Q + N (+ subordinate clause)

(37)   Q + art + N

(38)   Q + gen + N

(39)   Q + dem + N

(40)   dem + Q + N

(c) the same element cannot apparently be repeated e.g. dem + dem + N or Q + Q + N. Other combinations which do not seem possible are art + dem + N or dem + art + N.

6.10 (a) The phrase is an NP; it can be replaced by *it* and it begins with a genitive NP. But *acknowledging* looks like a verb (it is preceded by an adverb phrase and followed directly by an NP, unlike a noun). (b) A tree structure might be:

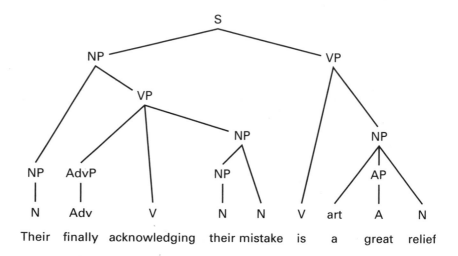

6.11 A working tree structure for this sentence has a headless noun phrase containing a relative clause.

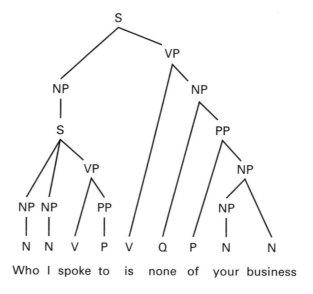

CHAPTER 7 ROOT SENTENCE AND SUBORDINATE CLAUSES

7.1

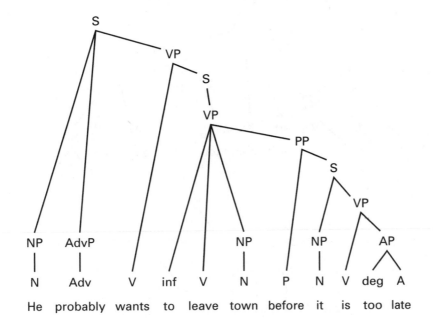

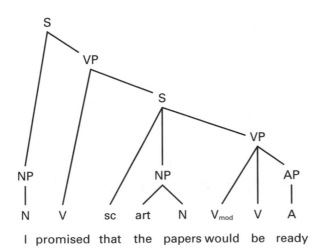

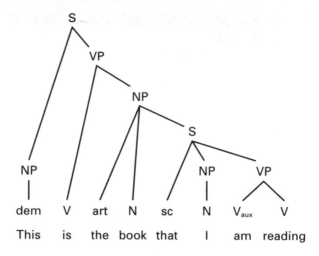

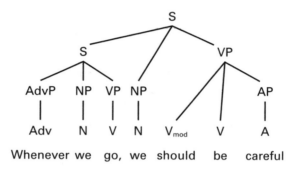

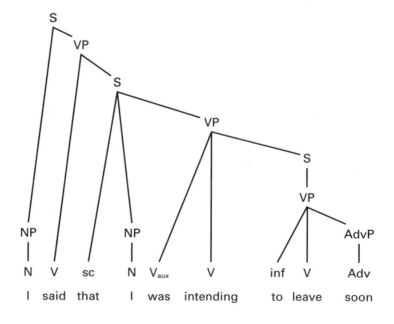

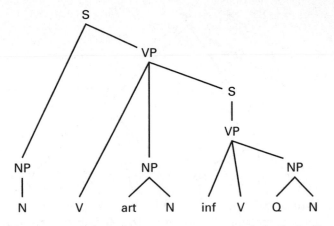

Mary persuaded the woman to read both books

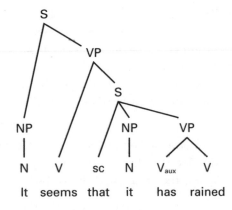

It seems that it has rained

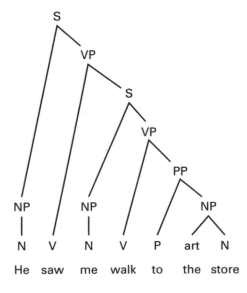

He saw me walk to the store

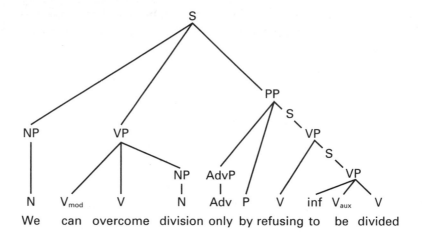

We can overcome division only by refusing to be divided

7.3   (a) (73) and (75) have *me* in the root clause; the subordinate clause is *to eat it* and can be substituted on its own, as in *She persuaded me that I should eat it* or *To eat it was what she told me*. (74) has *me* in the subordinate clause; the sentence can be rewritten as *she wanted that I should eat it*. (76) has *me* in the root clause but here it is not the subject of *eat*; instead *she* is identified as the subject of *eat*.

7.4   (a) Because it can be followed directly by an NP the verb *reading* must be a verb. Because the words *running* and *reading* 'head' subordinate clauses, they must both be verbs.

7.8   (a) *Nevertheless* and *therefore* roam free in the sentence and are thus analysable as adverbs. *In fact* is a PP.

7.10 One test: *because Mary left* can be moved around within the root clause; *and Mary left* cannot.

7.11 *The weather nice* can be replaced by a subordinate clause *the weather to be nice*. This suggests that it is a consituent and is itself a subordinate clause, even though it lacks a verb. (A verbless subordinate clause of this kind is sometimes called a 'small clause'.)

CHAPTER 8   MEANING AND FORM

8.2   (a) The verbs which cannot be followed by two NPs are (for most speakers) *donate, demonstrate, transfer, convey*. (b) Based on this list, these are the verbs of more than one syllable.

8.4   *Get* is clearly a verb because of its morphology. The problem is: is it an auxiliary verb or a main verb which takes a subordinate clause *read a lot*? The simplest analysis makes it an auxiliary, but it is unusual as an auxiliary: for example it does not invert with the subject in yes-no questions, it cannot be followed by *not* etc.

8.5   Your problem is to decide whether or not *see* is a verb or is a different class of word which happens to be a homophone with the verb *see*. One possibility is that *see* is used here as a preposition. (Compare: *As for the cappucino, does it have sugar in it?*)

8.6   In (36) *a very large parcel* is the object of the verb and would normally come immediately after it. In (37) the subordinate clause beginning *who* is the modifier of *girl* and so would be expected to be inside the subject noun phrase. In (38) *that this was a good idea* is interpretable as the subject of the sentence, replaced by *it* and displaced to the end.

8.7   You will find that the main verb *be* can always move; in some dialects the main verb *have* can move as in *Have you any money?* You may also find that verbs expressing movement can move; *Went the day well?*

8.8   The main difference from root questions is that here there is no placement of a tensed verb such as *do* before the subject. The word class of *that* might be a subordinating conjunction (it is homophonous with one); it might also be a demonstrative, which would fit better with the fact that it is substituting for a NP.

8.9   (b) In (47) and (48) *how slowly* is an adverb phrase and *how nice* is an adjective phrase and in both cases *how* is a degree modifier; in (49) *how* is an adjective phrase (it is replaced in answering the question with an adjective phrase), but it could be treated as a headless adjective phrase containing just the degree modifier *how* and no adjective. This would give a uniform account of *how*. (c) Justification for saying that the *how* phrase has moved includes (i) analogy with *wh*-movement, (ii) the fact that the *how* phrases are substituted in answers by material which follows rather than precedes the verb.

INDEX